REACHING BEYOND BOUNDARIES

REACHING BEYOND BOUNDARIES

A NAVY SEAL'S GUIDE TO ACHIEVING EVERYTHING YOU'VE EVER IMAGINED

DON MANN AND KRAIG BECKER

Skyhorse Publishing

Skyhorse Publishing books may be purchased in bulk at special discounts for sales promotion, corporate gifts, fund-raising, or educational purposes. Special editions can also be created to specifications. For details, contact the Special Sales Department, Skyhorse Publishing, 307 West 36th Street, 11th Floor, New York, NY 10018 or info@skyhorsepublishing.com.

Skyhorse® and Skyhorse Publishing® are registered trademarks of Skyhorse Publishing, Inc.®, a Delaware corporation.

Visit our website at www.skyhorsepublishing.com.

10 9 8 7 6 5 4 3 2 1

Library of Congress Cataloging-in-Publication Data is available on file.

Cover design by Brian Peterson

Print ISBN: 978-1-5107-3667-2
Ebook ISBN: 978-1-5107-3668-9

Printed in the United States of America.

CONTENTS

Chapter 1

PUSHING BEYOND BOUNDARIES

"Dream big and dare to fail."

—Norman Vaughn

High on a mountaintop in the Himalayas, a lone climber slowly scrambles up a steep slope. Strong winds buffet his body as he struggles to stand upright, snow swirling around him, obscuring his vision. His legs burn with exertion and his lungs struggle to provide the oxygen he needs in the increasingly thinning air. For a moment, he stops as a voice inside his head tells him that this would all be a lot easier if he just turned around and headed back down. He allows himself the briefest of moments to consider that possibility. Below him is warmth and sunshine, a comfortable tent, and the camaraderie of friends and family. Above, is only pain and suffering. He sighs deeply, drawing in even more oxygen before looking over his shoulder at the way he has come. Ultimately, he turns to continue upward. He hasn't finished what he has come here to do just yet. He hasn't reached the summit.

Somewhere on a desolate, sandy plateau in Afghanistan, a soldier ducks for cover behind an armored vehicle. A dozen rounds whiz past overhead as chaos breaks out all around him. He can see the other members of his squad scrambling for safety as bullets rain down from multiple directions. He takes a fraction of a second to collect himself, allowing his breathing and heart rate to stabilize. Adrenaline courses through his veins and yet he remains calm. "This is what we've trained for," he tells himself, glancing around to take stock of the situation and assess where his skills and experience are needed most. Without hesitation he begins scanning the area for signs of the enemy, conveying vital information to his fellow soldiers as the firefight escalates around him. Even in this life or death situation, he is calm and collected.

On a lonely trail in the Alps a runner pushes on through the night. She is sixteen hours and seventy miles into one of the longest and most difficult endurance events in the world. The route ahead is illuminated only by the light from her headlamp and it has been a long time since she has seen another living soul. Exhausted, hungry, and in pain, she presses forward, long after most other human beings would have stopped. The steepest and hardest part of the race is yet to come, but she refuses to give up now, as there are many miles to go before she reaches the finish line.

These grueling scenarios may sound like something out of a work of fiction, but they are the kind of real life challenges that men and women undertake all the time. Some choose to push themselves to their absolute physical and mental limits while others have intense, life-altering situations thrust upon them unexpectedly. But knowing how to embrace those moments, compartmentalize the suffering, and stay focused on achieving your objectives can be the difference between success and failure—and in some cases life and death.

I've spent the last forty years of my life vigorously preparing my mind, body, and soul to take on some of the most intense challenges imaginable. I've gone through arduous training so that I could defend my country against lethal threats from around the globe. I've conducted missions in places like Afghanistan, Iraq, Somalia, Yemen, El Salvador, Bolivia, Korea, Panama, and Colombia, often in conditions that were brutally demanding, both physically and mentally. To my SEAL teammates I am known as Warrant Officer Manslaughter, Sweet Satan, Don Maniac, and Dr. Death. All nicknames that I wear like a badge of honor, having served multiple tours of duty with SEAL Teams One, Two, and Six throughout my career.

My story starts in Methuen, Massachusetts, where I grew up a skinny kid from the wrong side of the tracks. As a teenager I was a hell-raiser with no interest in school or organized sports of any kind. Like most of my friends, I was on a one-way path to becoming a criminal or drug addict. It was then that I realized that if I didn't find some purpose in my life, I'd end up in prison, or dead. A number of my tough-guy friends—and even one of my girlfriends—had preceded me to an early grave. I was constantly getting into fights and running into trouble with the law. Needless to say, the prospects for my future weren't particularly bright.

To make matters worse, I was a terrible student. For me, school was nothing more than a place to hang out and have a good time. Some years I never even bothered to study at all. When our textbooks were issued on the first day of class, I'd stash them in my locker, and wouldn't look at them again until the last day of school when they needed to be returned. Once, as the end of the school year drew near, a teacher asked for her textbooks back and I remember telling her, "I'm sure they're in good condition, but they're in my locker, and I don't remember where my locker is."

After barely finishing high school, and graduating near the very bottom of my class, I wasn't really sure what my next move should be. But, I knew I had to do something, so I decided to enroll at a community college in Waterbury, Connecticut. I thought maybe I'd be well suited to becoming a policeman, telling myself that cops saw lots of action and got to carry weapons. I could be like my hero Evel Knievel who had switched from black leather to white, telling kids to stay in school and not do drugs, while still managing to remain a complete badass at the same time. So I signed up for a course in criminal justice and prepared myself for what I thought would be a good career path.

On the first day of class, the professor came into the classroom, looked around and asked, "How many of you here think you want to become cops?"

Practically everyone in the room—myself included—raised our hands. Then he said, "You want to be cops because of what you see on TV. The car chases, the shootouts. Isn't that right?"

A bunch of us answered, "You bet!" while shaking our heads enthusiastically.

"Well, those things will never happen," the professor told us. "You pull your weapon from your holster, and you're in court the next day defending yourself. The hours are terrible. So is the pay. The divorce rate is the highest of all civilian jobs. You spend most of your time writing parking tickets."

It was if all of the air had been left out of the classroom. We all looked at each other confused and dumbfounded. This wasn't what we had signed up for at all. Writing parking tickets for a living sounded mind-numbingly boring. My dream shattered, I had to find another profession, but the question was, what could that possibly be?

At that point in my life, I had been racing motocross bikes for several years and had demonstrated a real passion and knack for the sport. At one point I'd even been able to attract a sponsor in the form of Dave McCullen, the owner of the New Haven Suzuki motorcycle dealership. During a hotly-contested race in New Hampshire, I accidentally crashed headlong into Dave, breaking his leg in the process. Needless to say, that was the end of the sponsorship.

That wasn't the only motorcycle mishap I experienced while racing. I also managed to break all of the ribs on my right side, gotten bone fragments embedded in my liver, fractured my skull and right arm, broke several bones in my face and suffered a major concussion that left me in a coma for a week. It didn't take long to realize that racing motorcycles wasn't a career choice with a lot of growth potential.

Deciding that discretion was indeed the better part of valor, I abandoned my plans to become a professional motocross rider and enlisted in the Navy instead. It seemed like the right outlet to channel my energy, and it gave me a chance to go out and potentially do big things. It also allowed me to follow in the footsteps of my father who had also served in the Navy.

A few months prior to joining the service I had taken up running and weight lifting in order to get into better shape and to become a better motocross racer. I got off to a bit of a rocky start with my exercise regime, but before long I was working out every day and it soon became part of my daily routine. I'd even run several marathons, getting my time under two hours and fifty minutes. As I embarked on my training for the Navy, I was not only in great shape, but I was quickly starting to realize that if I pushed myself, I could accomplish great things in life.

It was about that time that I saw a training film about the Navy SEALs. I learned that SEAL stood for sea, air, and land, and that these elite warriors worked in small units and trained to perform the most difficult missions that the military had to offer. They went through intense training that allowed them to conduct operations in any type of environment—from deserts to frozen mountain peaks to jungles, and even urban settings. I thought, *Now that's the job for me!*

In order to become a SEAL you must first complete a rigorous six-month training program called BUD/S, which stands for Basic Underwater Demolition/SEAL. I'd heard that about 90 percent of the people who start the course drop out due to the tremendous mental and physical demands placed upon them. But because I wanted to be a SEAL more anything else, I trained hard to prepare myself for the challenges that I would face. I was determined to make it through, and eventually I did just that. It wasn't easy, and at times I was pushed to my absolute limits, but along the way I learned a lot about myself and where exactly my own personal boundaries were defined. I also learned how to go beyond those boundaries from time to time in order to achieve the objectives that I had set for myself.

It wasn't until I joined the Navy, and set my focus on becoming a SEAL, that I managed to set my life on a positive trajectory. It was then that I learned the value of discipline, training, and setting personal goals. This became a mindset that would eventually allow me to succeed not only as a SEAL, but in other aspects of my life too, instilling in me the ability to shrug off fear and doubt and press forward even in the face of overwhelming adversity.

I've witnessed shootings, decapitations, and stabbings. I've been taken prisoner twice but managed to escape and evade capture, returning to duty just days later. I've served as a SEAL jungle survival, desert survival, and arctic survival instructor; small arms weapons instructor; foreign weapons instructor; armed and unarmed defense tactics; advanced hand-to-hand combat instructor; and Survival, Evade, Resistance, and Escape instructor. In these roles, I've helped shape the minds and bodies of countless operatives, including several of the men who conducted the daring raid that led to the death of Osama Bin Laden.

Today, even though I've retired from the SEAL Teams, I continue to train some of our country's most elite warriors and athletes, as well as various government agency personnel. Dozens of times a year I'm invited to talk to business, civic, and athletic groups about something I call "Reaching beyond Boundaries." I talk to them about developing the mental toughness needed to perform at the top of their abilities under difficult circumstances. What I tell them is that their learning and training never ends, and that the boundaries that we think are confining us are more often than not self-imposed.

It is my belief that when setting our own personal goals we typically aim too low, usually out of fear and self-doubt. I also firmly believe that mental, physical, and spiritual discipline can give us the confidence we need to blow past any barriers that stand in our way. Whether we're competing in sports, business, or facing any of life's other myriad of challenges, knowing how to approach an objective and tackle roadblocks is a crucial part of achieving our goals. From leading men into combat, to managing a successful business, to completing a marathon, properly assessing our own true boundaries and learning how to move beyond them is often the key to success.

In addition to the many missions I've trained for and have been deployed on, I've also competed in over a thousand endurance competitions and ultra-distance athletic events in nearly every corner of the globe. Those competitions include Ironman and Double Ironman triathlons, as well as the legendary Raid Gauloises, an adventure race so tough it has been called the world's most difficult human endurance event. Adventure races like the Raid take place over days and often cover hundreds of miles, bringing endurance sports to an entirely different level. To me, they are the toughest competitions in the world, demanding the very best from any athlete. Naturally, I was drawn to them like a moth to a flame.

Without question I'm a bit of a physical training fanatic. One of my favorite mottos is "blood from any orifice." No one will ever accuse me of discounting the importance of physical training. I love it and do it every day of the year—rain or shine. Whether I'm running, swimming, biking, paddling, or lifting weights, the day simply isn't complete until I've managed to work in some form of physical exercise. For decades I have honed my strength and endurance, preparing to face the next challenge, no matter what form that challenge might appear. In fact, at one point in my life, I worked out for more than twenty-one years straight, without a day off—something that I am incredibly proud of.

I believe that a person can learn a lot about themselves while training for—and competing in—a running, cycling, paddling, or other type of endurance event. Often times, it isn't until we've taken ourselves to the absolute brink that we can identify where our boundaries actually lie and gain the confidence we need to push through them. Endurance sports can be the perfect environment for exploring those boundaries and redefining what we are capable of achieving.

With this book, we will examine ways that you too can push through the boundaries that you've set for yourself. We'll talk about setting goals and how to achieve them, while also developing a mental toughness that can get you through just about any challenge. We'll also share a number of thrilling real-life examples of this kind of mental toughness as it has been utilized by men and women during combat situations, in life or death survival scenarios, while embarking into the unknown, and during some of the most extreme sporting events in the world. These are all areas where mental toughness can be an asset that is even more important than physical gifts and intensive training.

It has been my experience that dedication, determination, and a razor sharp focus can make up for a lack of natural physical gifts. With the right mindset, an athlete of average talent can compete on the same playing field with someone who has been blessed with all of the physical gifts imaginable but lacks discipline and mental toughness. It is a way for a guy like Tom Brady to develop into arguably the greatest quarterback in NFL history, even if he isn't the strongest, fastest, or biggest player on the field.

Brady's story is a familiar one by now. Coming out of the University of Michigan back in 2000, he was viewed by NFL scouts as a solid college quarterback who played hard, made good decisions, and limited his mistakes. But he wasn't particularly fast, his arm strength was questionable, and if you passed him on the street you probably wouldn't have any idea that he was a college athlete. As a result, six other quarterbacks were picked ahead of him, including a guy by the name of Giovanni Carmazzi who played college ball for the relatively unknown Hofstra University. Carmazzi was taken in the third round by the San Francisco 49ers, but would end up never playing a single down in the NFL. Still, he was drafted ahead of Brady who waited patiently to hear his name called.

The New England Patriots finally selected Brady in the sixth round with the 199th pick overall. He would have to wait a year before he actually got a chance to play in a meaningful game, taking the field in relief of injured starter Drew Bledsoe in week two of the 2001 season. But once he actually managed to get some playing time, Brady took control of the team and there was no turning back. The rest is history.

There is no denying that Brady is a hell of a quarterback, but he hasn't been blessed with the same physical gifts of some of his contemporaries. Other QBs are faster, more mobile, and have stronger arms. That hasn't mattered one bit however, as he has shown time and again that he is practically unflappable on the field, has supreme confidence in his own abilities, and is as mentally tough as anyone who has ever played the game. As a result, he has gone on to win five Super Bowls and was named the MVP in four of those games.

At the other end of that spectrum of Brady is a man like Reinhold Messner. He's not exactly a household name, but he is definitely a hero of mine. Raised in the Italian Dolomites, Messner is considered by many to be the greatest mountaineer of all time. His list of accomplishments is long and distinguished. But perhaps most impressively, in 1978 he and his climbing partner Pater Habler proved skeptics wrong by summiting Mt. Everest without the use of bottled oxygen. At the time, experts thought that was akin to going to the moon without a spacesuit. Not content with completely changing the accepted paradigms of mountaineering however, Messner would return two years later to do it again, this time completely on his own. That expedition would become the first ever solo summit of Everest, a feat that has yet to be truly matched to this day.

No one questions Messner's physical gifts. In his prime, he was a mountaineer without equal. But, in addition to having incredible strength and stamina, he was also as mentally tough as they come. He could endure the harshest weather conditions imaginable, sometimes spending days confined to a tent while he waited for conditions to improve. Through it all, he remained focused and determined, which is what often truly set him apart from his peers. His unwavering faith in his own abilities and his willingness to push through his personal boundaries were the traits that enabled him to go to great heights, both literally and figuratively.

The Italian alpinist was a master at setting seemingly-impossible goals and then figuring out ways to make them a reality. Often he would imagine every detail of an expedition ahead of time, planning and plotting his approach, overcoming some of the biggest obstacles long before he ever set foot on a mountain. This mental preparation was an important part of Messner's process, and a major key to his success. He could visualize every stage of the journey, breaking it down into smaller, more manageable segments, then he would put all the pieces together so that he could successfully reach the summit. The goal was always to climb the mountain, but it was a series of smaller objectives, much more manageable on an individual level, that allowed him to eventually achieve the larger one.

I refer to this as macro- and micro-goal setting and it is an important aspect of pushing beyond our personal boundaries. Throughout this book, we'll discuss such topics as setting monumental challenges (macro goals) for ourselves, and then finding smaller objectives (micro goals) that can serve as the stepping stones to success. We'll discuss how to get yourself into the right mindset to take on a challenge and overcome adversity when it inevitably rears its ugly head. We'll look at the ways that we can learn from both our successes and failures, and we'll talk about what it takes to eliminate excuses and keep moving forward, no matter what life throws our way.

We'll also examine the value of constantly learning new things and finding new adventures to pursue, no matter what stage of our lives we are in. As the old saying goes, complacency is the enemy of success, and I believe that there is no better way to stay young than challenging yourself in new and interesting ways. Having objectives to pursue can help keep your mind and body sharp, and when you start to realize all of the things that you can accomplish, you'll begin to set your sights even higher. Confidence can play a big role in achieving your goals and it can lead to even bigger things down the line when it is mixed with experience.

Perhaps most importantly of all, we'll even discuss how to identify when you are pushing yourself too hard and how to back off, allowing yourself time to recover and regroup. This can help you to avoid burnout, stay focused, and keep connected with the important people in your life too. After all, what good is achieving the big goals that you set for yourself if you have to give up everything else along the way? We're here to talk about how to build an adventurous, successful life, not destroy it.

Over the course of the following chapters I'll share more stories from my own life and career as a Navy SEAL and endurance athlete. I'll also provide some inspiring—and sometimes harrowing—tales of others who have been able to push beyond their own personal boundaries and literally redefine what we know humans beings are capable of achieving. Those stories will come from a variety of different areas, including adventure sports, mountaineering, exploration, and business. Hopefully these tales will prove equal parts entertaining and educational, serving as examples of the concepts and philosophies that we'll be discussing.

Whether you're looking for motivation to set some new goals and then go after them, or you already have some major objectives you'd like to achieve in mind, I hope to provide a blueprint that can help you get to where you want to go. I believe that we can accomplish just about anything that we set our minds to, provided we are in the right mindset, are willing to work hard, and are willing to push ourselves out of our comfort zone from time to time, too.

This book is a template for how to make that happen while

getting to know yourself better along the way. Hopefully, by the end, you'll have the tools you need to reach your goals and to achieve things you might not have even dreamed were possible. These are the tactics that have worked for me and I think they'll work for you too.

REINHOLD MESSNER
Mountaineer

When it comes to high-altitude mountaineering, no one has been able to push himself further or to greater heights than Italian climber Reinhold Messner. Born and raised in the South Tyrol region of Italy back in 1944, Messner cut his teeth climbing in the Alps and the Dolomites at a very young age. What he learned there would not only allow him to go on to make history on the most demanding peaks on the planet, but also completely shift what we thought was possible in the mountains.

I first learned about Reinhold Messner while sitting in a dentist office at the Naval Regional Medical Center in Rhode Island. While there, I causally picked up an issue of *Sports Illustrated* and started thumbing through the articles. As I turned the pages, I came across a story about Messner, who the author called "the greatest mountaineer in history." Up until that point, I had never heard of him, but later I would come to learn as much as I could about this enigmatic man, and he has inspired me every day since.

While reading the *SI* story I learned that in June of 1970 Reinhold Messner set out on his very first Himalayan expedition. But instead of proceeding in the usual "expedition style" using yaks, fixed ropes, and Sherpa guides, he decided to assault the world's highest mountains in what is called "alpine style." This meant he would be carrying everything he needed on his back and would do all of the work himself, a feat completely unheard of at the time. It also meant he would make his ascent without the use of Sherpa support or guides and in a lighter, faster fashion. He wanted to climb in what he called "the fairest means possible," meaning he wouldn't take any shortcuts or use outside assistance along the way.

And if that wasn't challenging enough, his goal was to be the first man to summit the highest sheer rock face in the world—the

15,000-foot ice-covered Rupal Face on Nanga Parbat. The Italian's plan was to make the first complete traverse of the mountain too, climbing to the summit along this impossibly difficult route, then descending along the Diamir Face, which at that time was virtually unexplored. It was a bold plan to say the least and most other professional mountaineers thought he was delusional.

Messner ended up proving them all wrong however, accomplishing everything he set out to do and more. But in doing so, he ended up paying a heavy price—losing his brother in an avalanche on the descent and suffering severe frostbite in his feet that ended up claiming seven of his toes.

Prior to his Himalayan debut on Nanga Parbat, Messner had earned a reputation as an amazing climber in the Alps, making more than five hundred ascents throughout his younger years. It was there that he honed his skills and learned to push his boundaries, testing the limits of his physical and mental toughness. Those were things that would serve him well on later expeditions, where his already-impressive skills and endurance would be tested to their limits.

Eight years after his dramatic ascent of Nanga Parbat, Messner would make history in a completely new way. With just three toes remaining, he and his teammate Peter Habeler would become the first climbers to summit Mt. Everest without the use of oxygen tanks. Up until that point, nearly everyone thought that such a feat was impossible due to the severe lack of oxygen at such high altitudes.

Climbing anywhere above 26,000 feet is considered "the death zone" because the human body begins to shut down and consume itself in the extremely thin air. All prior expeditions to such heights required climbers to wear oxygen masks and heavy tanks. But Messner and Habeler were able to prove that man could exist at such altitudes for a short time and return back down the mountain safely.

The ascent was a difficult one for the two men who struggled with every step. On more than one occasion, as they approached the summit, the duo collapsed to the ground, struggling to continue as their bodies tried to desperately take in air. But they continued upward nonetheless, putting one foot in front of the other, despite every fiber in their being begging them to stop, turn around, and head down. In the end, they were successful however, and the mountaineering world was changed forever.

Two years later, Messner would make history on Everest once again when he made the first solo ascent of that mountain. That meant that he climbed completely alone, without Sherpa support or even teammates to provide assistance. Once again, he didn't use bottled oxygen, which added yet another element to this remarkable feat. He even arrived on the mountain fully acclimatized and ready to climb, making the ascent in just four days. Typically an Everest expedition requires more than a month to complete.

It is nearly impossible to express just how difficult a solo summit of Everest truly is, particularly back in 1980—well before commercial expedition companies opened the mountain to many more people. Messner's expedition stands as perhaps the greatest feat in mountaineering history, but for the Italian climber it was just the next goal he had set for himself.

But Messner wasn't finished leaving his mark on mountaineering just yet. Having conquered Everest and Nanga Parbat, along with several other major peaks, he decided to set yet another goal for himself. He wanted to become the first person to climb all of the world's 8,000-meter peaks. In total, there are fourteen such mountains, and at that point in history no one had even come close to summiting all of them.

In 1986, Messner became the first person to accomplish that goal, knocking off most of the remaining mountains in alpine style and without the use of supplemental oxygen. That same year he would also complete a modified version of the Seven Summits, during which he climbed the highest mountain on each of the seven continents.

There is no denying Messner's impact on mountaineering. He set the gold standard for all other climbers that have followed, while also proving that human beings could do things that no one had ever imagined before. In redefining our expectations, he continued to set the bar higher not only for every other climber on the planet, but for himself too. It was no longer enough to just go out and lay siege to a mountain, overcoming it with brute force. Messner introduced a more subtle, elegant approach to climbing, one where man and nature were on more equal terms and expeditions were undertaken in the purest style imaginable.

Messner is an individual who continually looked for new challenges; he didn't just find them in the mountains. Throughout his illustrious career he also become the first person to cross Antarctica and Greenland without using a motorized vehicle or a dogsled. He also managed to trek the length of the Gobi Desert completely on his own as well, once again finding solace and inspiration in the most remote corners of the planet.

Reading about Messner's exploits I was completely fascinated and inspired. The Italian is practically the human embodiment of the type of heroic individual I wanted to become—one who didn't accept limitations and redefined the word "courage." Someone who set goals most experts considered unreachable, and then went on to crush them. Over and over again he defied expectations, finding ways to dig deep within himself to accomplish great things on a continual basis.

Messner is pretty much the living example of what it means to push beyond boundaries. In his pursuit of mountaineering greatness he learned to ignore pain and suffering in order to achieve the objectives that he set for himself. Climbing the world's toughest peaks without using oxygen was something that no one thought was possible, but he willed himself to the summit of Everest nonetheless, his lungs burning and legs aching the entire way. In doing so, he completed a paradigm shift that reverberated across the mountaineering community and continues to inspire climbers to this day.

When looking over Messner's list of accomplishments it is nearly impossible not to be impressed. His achievements are unmatched in the mountaineering world and there will likely never be another climber of his caliber. It was his exploits on the highest peaks in the world that inspired me to start climbing as well, eventually leading to my own attempt on Everest. His mental toughness and physical endurance are practically unmatched, making him a role model to an entire generation of mountaineers who followed him, myself included.

Chapter 2

THE COMBAT MINDSET

"Once you learn to quit, it becomes a habit."
—Vince Lombardi

I've quit twice in my life, and both times I felt absolutely miserable for a long period of time afterwards. In both cases, I also gained a deep understanding of myself and came away motivated to never feel that way again.

The first of those experiences came when I was still in high school, trying to figure out what I wanted to do with my life. I'd been racing motocross for a while and even though I had managed to seriously injure myself on more than one occasion, I was still pondering the idea of turning professional.

One day, my friend Dave Kelleher—who was a professional motocross rider—told me that if I wanted to get serious about racing, I needed to start training. I respected his opinion, but wasn't sure what he was getting at.

"Training? What do you mean, Dave? I'm at the track all the time." I asked a bit incredulously.

"I'm talking about physical training," he answered. "Working out. I run ten miles, three times a week."

At that point, I'd never run in my life. I hadn't even considered it, or how it could help me with racing motorcycles. But, I eagerly agreed to join Dave for a workout and the next morning I met him at his house in New Haven, Connecticut. Dave had measured a one-mile loop in his neighborhood that he ran ten times. I completed the first mile with him at a leisurely pace, but really did not enjoy it. Throughout that first mile I was feeling a bit uncomfortable with my legs and lungs crying for relief. The second mile was worse than the first and by mile three, I was breathing harder than ever. I thought I was going to throw up so I just quit running, plopped down on the grass, and watched David push himself to complete the ten mile run. Every mile he looked more and more exhausted.

When Dave passed on his sixth mile, I said to myself, *I'm watching a professional motocross racer get fitter and stronger, and I'm just sitting here on the grass because I'm a quitter and don't know how to push myself.* As I watched him complete the tenth, and final lap, I felt completely pathetic. I asked myself, *how am I going to become good at anything if when I start to feel a little uncomfortable I just quit?* It was a damn good question.

The next day, I started running and working out. It became my new mission in life to improve my physical conditioning and every night, I spent hours lifting weights in my bedroom with the Rolling Stones or Black Sabbath blaring through my headphones. I'd try to do a continuous set of a particular exercise—curls, bench presses, overhead presses, push-ups, or sit-ups to an individual song without stopping.

A couple of months later I went back to work out with Dave, and this time I was able to stay with him. It felt great, not only because I ran as fast as my friend who I respected so much, but because I had come so far in such a short period of time. I also learned that I loved exercising and pushing my body to its limits, which I was only just starting to discover.

Four months after that, I ran the Boston Marathon. It was painful as hell, but I promised myself that I wouldn't stop running until I crossed the finish line. Bill Rodgers won the race that year with a time of two hours, nine minutes, and fifty-five seconds. I did cross the finish line, but in a time of three hours and forty-four minutes.

I told myself that at least I'd finished and just as I promised myself, I did not walk at any point throughout the race. I had run the entire length of one of the most prestigious marathons in the world.

But I wasn't content with my performance and knew I could get better. I was determined to get stronger and faster. I trained hard every day. A month later, when I ran a second marathon, my time was down to 3:33. By the time I ran my third marathon, I shaved an additional seventeen minutes off my time and finished in the top 20 percent. A month later, I clocked in at three hours and six minutes.

My next goal was to beat three hours. A couple weeks after that, I did, crossing the finish line at two hours, fifty minutes. I ended up running thirty marathons or ultra-marathons in just three years. That's a blistering pace for any athlete. It was about then that I realized something very important: if you push yourself hard enough, you can accomplish things you didn't think you were capable of. Maybe even great things.

I ended up putting my goal of becoming a professional motocross racer aside when I joined the Navy. My plan was to work out a lot and race motocross on the weekends I had free. My recruiter led me to believe I would have plenty of weekends off and I could do whatever I wished in my own off-duty time. Well, as it turned out, I traveled or worked most weekends and my hopes and chances of earning enough points at races to go pro were increasingly unlikely.

At that point in my life I was still working out every day and competing in marathons, bike races, and even my first Ironman competition in Hawaii. I was in the best shape of my life and constantly looking for new challenges. I'd get all the challenge I'd ever want, and then some, when I began my Basic Underwater Demolition/ SEAL training. It was there that I'd also feel the sting of quitting once again too.

The first two months of the program (First Phase) consisted of timed runs in the sand, calisthenics, small boat seamanship, hydrographic surveys, and swimming. Our BUD/S instructors had a quick method of testing our response. They'd tie our hands behind our backs, bind our feet, and then toss us in the pool.

Some of us figured out that the only way to avoid drowning was to relax, sink to the bottom of the pool, kick off powerfully towards the surface, get our lips above the water line, gasp for a bit of air, then drop to the bottom again.

Others panicked, swallowed water, coughed, choked, and even eventually passed out. Once divers retrieved those individuals from the bottom of the pool, the unconscious trainees were rolled on their sides and were revived. Then, instructors screamed in their faces, "Are you gonna quit? Did you get uncomfortable? What are you wasting your time for, quitter? You want to quit now?"

They were given thirty seconds to answer before they were tossed out of the program. Lots of guys left voluntarily.

Those who said they wanted to keep going were thrown back in the pool. The ones who refused to give up, who could suppress the need to breathe, who trusted that they'd be rescued if something went wrong and were prepared to lose consciousness ultimately passed. The instructors called it drown-proofing.

During one exercise we had to stand on the side of the pool, do a forward flip into the water, then complete a 50-meter swim underwater without coming up for air.

When it came to my turn, I did my flip and swam 25 meters, reaching the far wall, and executed my flip-turn and started back. At that point it felt like an ice pick was going through my head as my lungs started to burn with the exertion. I wanted to breathe so badly. The feeling that I needed air became so intense, I just shot to the surface to suck in some oxygen. Almost immediately an instructor shouted, "You quitter! Get out of the pool and stand over there with the other quitters!"

Feeling about two inches tall, I got out and joined the majority of my classmates along the side of the pool. We stood there sheepishly, looking for a place to hide, as eight of our compatriots completed the swim as required. As they hauled themselves out of the water, the instructor shouted to the eight who had passed, "You see those losers over there? They quit. You want to go to war with those quitters? They were feeling a little uncomfortable and had to come up to breathe. The hell with them. We can't allow lower than whale-shit quitters to continue on with training."

As tough as the instructors were on us, I was even harder on myself. *What the hell's wrong with you? Just because you were a little uncomfortable you had to come up for air? That's pathetic!* All I did for the previous four years was to train for BUD/S. I wanted nothing else in life but to be a SEAL. I felt as though when I quit, my life was over. It had no meaning at all. I couldn't believe I felt a little uncomfortable, a little bad for myself, and I just quit again.

Meanwhile, a couple of the instructors huddled together and were talking. One of them then said, "Alright, let's give these quitters one more chance."

I told myself, *whatever happens, I'm not coming up for air. I don't care if my head explodes. I'm not quitting this time.* I jumped back into the water, swam to the far end, did my flip-turn, and started back. It wasn't long into my return trip across the pool that my lungs started to scream once again. The feeling that there was an ice pick in my brain was even worse this time around as I struggled to make my way through the water.

Remembering how it felt to come up short on my previous attempt, I forced myself to press onward. By that point, my entire body was pleading with me to rise to the surface and suck in some air, but I ignored those instincts. *You can do this,* I told myself as the wall drew nearer. *You have to do this.*

Later in my training I would learn that while you might think that you need air, in reality your body isn't lacking oxygen at all. Instead, it is the CO_2 receptors in your brain telling you that it's time to exhale and shed the carbon dioxide that has built up while you hold your breath. If you exhale just a little, you can easily last a minute or so longer.

But at that moment I hadn't acquired that particular skill, and as a result I blacked out in the water. I don't remember seeing or feeling the wall. All I know is that the safety divers pulled me out of the pool, and I heard one of the instructors say, "Okay, you passed."

That's all I wanted to hear. I wasn't kicked out of BUD/S and I had learned another valuable lesson. Quitting is never an option in the Teams. In fact, it would never cross my mind again. Even when I was injured, about to drown, or captured by the enemy, I never gave up. I learned that it was better to be tortured or to die, then to disgrace myself, my country, or my teammates.

I also realized that I was lucky enough to get a second chance, and I made the most of it. Not everyone is so fortunate. It was a good reminder to make the most of the opportunities that we are given, because they may not come around again.

Armed with this knowledge and my "don't ever quit" attitude, I went on to graduate from BUD/S. Of the 120 men that started with me, only twenty-three passed the course. It would be another six months before I was officially off probation and awarded my highly-coveted SEAL trident. That was one of the proudest days of my life. About four years after that came another proud day when I was selected for SEAL Team Six, the most elite of all the SEAL teams.

These experiences taught me that the most important weapon an individual can develop isn't thickly-muscled arms, powerful legs, or top-notch physical stamina. Sure, those things can be a benefit when you're in the thick of an intense situation. But it is a strong, positive, keenly focused, unwavering mental outlook—something we in the Teams call the Combat Mindset—will see you through the most difficult of challenges. It is something that highly successful people from all walks of life have, whether they are SEALs, endurance athletes, mountaineers, surgeons, accountants, or CEOs.

What is the Combat Mindset exactly? It's a state of mental toughness that enables you to shield out all distractions—including fear, doubt, and pain—and perform to your maximum abilities under the most dangerous and high-stake circumstances. And it is nothing less than a prerequisite for success on the battlefield, in the boardroom, or any form of physical undertaking or competition. It is a quality that some people are lucky enough to be born with, but it is also something that the rest of us can learn through hard work, training, dedication, and experience.

For me, the Combat Mindset is a tool that can see you through the most challenging and demanding undertakings of your life, and I'm not alone in that assessment. Retired US Army Lt. Colonel Dave Grossman specializes in the study of the psychology of combat, and has instructed cadets at West Point on that very subject. He tells his students that while skill and training are important, more often than not a strong mindset is the most important thing they need to survive combat.

In other words, no matter how much training and preparation a soldier receives, his or her ability to stay calm and focused under fire is the most important factor not only to their survival, but their chances of successfully completing a mission. This is a sentiment that I wholeheartedly agree with. In my years as a Navy SEAL, I used the Combat Mindset to get me through more than a dozen near-death experiences, both in training and during operations. I didn't know it at the time, but it was this mental toughness that helped me press on in the pool that day when every fiber of my body wanted to quit.

This is a subject that I feel is so important, that I've been talking about it for years not only to other SEALs, but also to endurance athletes, students, and business executives across the country. I tell them that when faced with extreme hardship and danger, I've seen tough, hard bodied 220-pound professional football players turn to mush when faced with adversity. I've also watched a fifty-year-old woman push herself beyond what most people would think was humanly possible. During an ultra-distance race in South Africa, this woman actually told me, "Don, I will not die on you. I might feel like I'm going to die. But I will not die. My body will eat from itself."

That is the very personification of Combat Mindset. It is all about recognizing that you are about to push yourself to your physical and mental limits, testing every fiber of your being along the way. But it is also about knowing that you are strong enough to actually survive—and possibly even thrive—under those conditions. Having a powerful Combat Mindset makes it possible to embrace suffering in a way that you never thought possible, while continuing to perform at an extremely high level.

Brigadier General Rhonda Cornum learned the importance of mental toughness during the First Gulf War. While serving in Iraq, she was part of a search and rescue operation sent out to find a downed F-16 pilot. During that mission the Black Hawk helicopter she was flying in came under fire, with a stray round striking her in the right shoulder. The helicopter sustained quite a bit of damage too, crash landing hard in the desert and knocking her unconscious.

During the crash she suffered two broken arms, a smashed knee, and a nasty cut over her eye. When she regained consciousness she quickly took stock of her injuries and assessed the situation. She was obviously in a great deal of pain but spotted several fires amongst the wreckage. Knowing that it was not safe to stay in the downed aircraft, she managed to drag herself out to safety. Later she would recall thinking to herself, "Nobody's ever died from pain."

Cornum's wounds left her in a vulnerable position and eventually led to her capture by the Iraqi Republican Guard, a unit well known for its brutality. Her captors placed her in the back of an old pickup truck for transport to a nearby outpost and while en route one of the enemy soldiers unzipped her flight suit and sexually assaulted her as she lay there helpless.

Over the course of the following week, Cornum was interrogated on multiple occasions and subjected to mock executions. Her captors excelled at playing mind games, convincing their prisoners that they could be killed at any time. On more than one occasion an Iraqi soldier held a gun to her head and pulled the trigger. The chamber was empty of course, but the physiological impact of never knowing if there was a bullet in the chamber took its toll.

Throughout that traumatic experience, the then-Major Cornum stayed calm, even though she was sure she would be killed. Later she would reveal that she kept telling herself "I've really had a great life—I've done almost all of what I wanted to do and I've accomplished more things than many people do who live twice as long as me."

A week later she was rescued and brought home. After the ordeal she continued to serve in the military and was eventually promoted to General. Cornum would also go on to head the US military's Comprehensive Soldier Fitness (CSF) program, which was created to help prepare troops for the psychic trauma of warfare. Designed at the University of Pennsylvania's Positive Psychology Center, it zeros in on five aspects of a soldier's psychological health: physical, emotional, social, family, and spiritual.

Founded in 2008, the idea behind the CSF was to give military personnel, their families, and civilians working within the armed forces the tools they needed to handle the ongoing stress of prolonged conflicts in Afghanistan and Iraq. The program introduced training procedures that were designed to help create a mental and emotional skillset that could prevent post-traumatic stress syndrome rather than dealing with those issues after the fact. The focus was to build mental toughness and resiliency amongst the troops. In other words, the idea was to instill in them the concepts that are integral to Combat Mindset.

Concurrent with the military's increased emphasis on mental fitness has been an entirely new focus on the psychology of combat. In the wake of the wars in Afghanistan and Iraq, countless military personnel have returned home only to struggle with the challenges of transitioning back to civilian life. Often those soldiers, sailors, and airmen are still dealing with the horrors of war, which contrasts sharply with the home front. This has led to more in-depth studies on the causes of post-traumatic stress disorder with some fascinating results. For instance, scientists now understand that in situations that manifest PTSD, stress hormones like adrenaline actually scorch the painful memories of an intense event deep into the parts of the brain that are responsible for the retention of long-term memories.

With suicide rates and incidences of post-traumatic stress among soldiers at an all-time high, the US military has come to the conclusion that giving our warfighters the tools they need to deal with intense situations is crucial in an era of sustained, protracted modern deployments in a combat zone. A colonel that I spoke with confirmed as much, saying, "We used to do PT five times a week, until I realized I wasn't losing soldiers because they couldn't run. I was losing them for other psychological issues. Now we spend an equal amount of time focusing on developing mental toughness."

Trainers in the Army's CSF program have learned the importance of teaching problem-solving, goal-setting, collaborative planning, energy management, and something General Cornum likes to call PIP—putting it in perspective—in preparing soldiers psychologically for the battlefield. In other words, understanding that although conditions might be bad, it could always be worse. These are principles that play an important role in developing a Combat Mindset as well.

Sometimes it's as simple as telling soldiers what to expect on the battlefield. According to Professor Grossman, "When a soldier knows what he's likely to face he'll be able to say, 'I was warned that might happen, no big deal,' then do some breathing and get it under control." Preparation and proper training automatically kick in to help the solider to remain calm and do his or her job, even while under fire.

In other cases, it's a matter of identifying those who are at high risk for PTSD and preparing them psychologically for the challenges of war. Dr. Donald Sandweiss, formerly of the Naval Health Research Center in San Diego, told me that studies have shown that soldiers with a prior history of depression, panic disorder, or other psychiatric illnesses are twice as likely to develop post-traumatic stress disorder. He said, "More vulnerable members of the deployed population benefit from interventions targeted to prevent or to ensure early identification and treatment of post-deployment PTSD."

In 2011, Dr. Sandweiss released the results of a study that included more than 22,000 soldiers. Those men and women were given a survey regarding the state of their mental health prior to departing for Iraq and Afghanistan, and then given that same survey when they returned home. That survey showed that about 3 percent suffered from some kind of mental health issue before ever being deployed. But after serving abroad, that number rose to 8 percent. Researchers found that those with a preexisting condition were more than twice as likely to develop PTSD while at war. The study also showed that while physical injuries sustained in combat sometimes played a role in creating post-traumatic stress, it was much less of factor than having a preexisting condition.

In the arena of Special Operations, candidates for selection to the Navy SEALs and US Army Special Forces are actually tested for their body's ability to deal with danger and extreme stress. It starts with something called heart rate variability, or HRV. Most healthy people have a lot of variation in the length of the intervals between beats, with their hearts speeding up and slowing down constantly. If they face a moment that excites or scares them, their heart rate is likely to elevate. In quieter, more relaxed moments, it tends to slow down.

Researchers have learned that the best Special Operations

candidates are those who have very little heart-rate variability. They have what are called "metronomic heartbeats," which is to say their hearts thump steadily, like metronomes, with almost no variability whatsoever no matter what is happening around them. This is because their bodies produce a higher level of an amino acid called neuropeptide Y (NPY), which helps regulate blood pressure, appetite, learning, and memory. It's also works as a natural tranquilizer, controlling anxiety and buffering the effects of stress hormones like norepinephrine, also known as noradrenaline. Essentially, NPY is used by the brain to block out alarm and fear responses and keep the frontal lobe working, even under extreme stress.

In some respects the military is still playing catch up with the sports community in this area. Athletes and coaches have long appreciated the importance of mental toughness and keeping a cool head in the midst of intense competition. As Lester Hamlin of the US Olympic Training Center explained, "We have understood for years that many elite athletes fail during competition because of a lack of mental control. One of the characteristics of Olympic champions is their ability to cope with and control anxiety."

Few people exhibit more control over fear and anxiety than rock climber Alex Honnold. As a free-soloist, Honnold often makes daring and difficult climbs without the use of ropes or any safety equipment whatsoever. Free soloing is the most dangerous form of climbing there is, with absolutely no room for error. When Honnold takes to the rock it is usually a matter of his skill, strength, and experience being put to the test on some of the most difficult climbing routes found anywhere in the world.

Case in point, in June of 2017 Alex stunned the world by making the first free solo ascent of El Capitan in Yosemite National Park, a massive granite face that stretches more than 3,000 feet into the air. When that giant rock wall was first climbed back in 1958, it took forty-seven days to scale its lofty heights with a trio of climbers employing dozens of ropes and safety equipment that was carefully fixed into place ahead of time. Honnold completed the climb in a remarkable three hours and fifty-six minutes, wearing just the clothes on his back, a pair of climbing shoes, and a chalk bag.

For most of us, the mere thought of climbing a 3,000-foot rock wall—with or without a rope—is enough to make us weak in the knees. In fact, the climb was so groundbreaking and terrifying that other rock climbers were shocked by Honnold's feat, with some openly joking about his state of mental health. Alex is perfectly sane of course, but it probably shouldn't come as a surprise to learn that his brain doesn't actually operate in the same way as a normal person's, particularly with how it processes stressful situations.

In 2016, researchers used an MRI to scan Alex's brain to record how it responded to disturbing images designed to evoke fear and discomfort. What they found was that his amygdala—the section of the brain that covers such activity—didn't fire on the same level as it would for most other people. He simply didn't react in the same way that many would when placed in situations that would typically be terrifying. The study showed that Honnold truly is the man without fear, which explains how he is able to push himself to great heights without so much as elevating his heart rate. The question is, was he born this way or did he achieve this Zen-like level of calm through training and experience? Odds are, it is a little bit of both.

This quality—the ability to cope with and control anxiety—is at the core of the Combat Mindset and often defines the difference between victory and defeat, success or failure, life and death. It's something all of us hope to achieve whether we're dealing with challenges on the battlefield, the mountain, the boardroom, or some other area of our lives. It is a state of mind that can be learned through hard work, understanding and focusing on specific goals.

Of course, not many people have a brain that processes fear and stress in the same way as Alex Honnold, nor are we all given specialized training by the military to help us cope with those emotions. Quite the contrary in fact, as most of us must learn how to deal with and confront our fears in our own personal way.

So how does one go about developing or strengthening a Combat Mindset? We'll be exploring that very topic in detail in the chapters that follow, but it all starts with consistency and perseverance in everything you do. If you want to run a marathon, you have to work out on a consistent basis. If you want to be successful in business, take a consistent approach to working towards your goals and always keep moving forward even when hit with a setback.

Mental toughness is forged in the fires of adversity and is honed to a fine edge through consistent effort, training, and learning. This is something that I've learned firsthand and seen in action on many occasions. Ultimately it can give you the tools to stay positive and focused, even when things can seem hopeless.

Here's an example of how the Combat Mindset served me well while on a mission that didn't quite go as planned. I can't reveal the specific place or the nature of the mission I was on, but I can tell you that I was in a village in Central America in territory controlled by leftist guerrillas, when I found myself running for my life. A military colleague of mine named Billy was beside me, trying to keep up, wheezing hard and sweating. A third colleague, Greg—the one who had compromised our mission—was somewhere behind us. We were hoping to find him while running for our lives at the same time.

We were unarmed and had soldiers, local policemen, and a good portion of the townspeople in hot pursuit. One of the policemen raised his handgun and shouted at us in Spanish to stop.

"What should we do, Don?" Billy asked.

It was extremely hot, the atmosphere was clogged with dust, and you could almost see the humidity hanging in the air. It was not a pleasant environment to be running through, but the last thing I wanted was to get caught. I shouted, "Billy, zigzag!"

We did just that, even though it probably wasn't necessary. There were far too many people watching from the windows and doorways of their houses and huts for the police to shoot without the risk of hitting someone with a stray round.

We sprinted down a dirty street, then cut through someone's front yard, ducking into a small mud and timber shack. Zipping past a woman preparing a meal in her kitchen, we continued out through a courtyard where children played and chickens squawked. In the backyard was a man tending to his little garden who was startled to find two Americanos rushing past.

It was about then that I looked over my shoulder. The angry mob chasing us had grown larger. They looked like they wanted to tear us apart. "This way, Billy!" I shouted, sweat pouring down my face, my heart pounding. I turned into another yard, climbed a fence, and crossed a little dirt parking lot. The cops and other villagers were still right on our heels.

Forty minutes later we were still running, but exhausted and thirsty, and I knew something had to change soon. It was right about then that I spotted a little saloon to our left and turned in with Billy right behind me. We tried to act cool as we slid onto a couple of stools at the bar, despite the fact that we were wheezing like race-horses, caked with dust, and dripping with sweat. It didn't help that we were the only white people in the joint either.

Between gasps of breath, Billy said, "Holy shit, Don! I can't be-lieve what just happened."

"Me, neither, Billy," I whispered back, trying to catch my breath.

"Where the hell is Greg?"

"Don't know," I said, "but I hope he escaped."

"What do we do now?"

I thought for a second and replied, "Order some *cervezas* and think."

The bartender stood at the opposite end of the bar talking to a mean-looking fellow and looking at us suspiciously. In the mirror behind the bar, I saw three more local men seated at a little table muttering to themselves. The door we had entered through was to our left. There was a second door on the right.

I said, "Billy, after we catch our breath, let's exit out the door behind us and on the right."

"Got it."

Looking in the mirror again, I saw three dark figures standing in the doorway. I couldn't tell if they were holding weapons or not but didn't want to wait around to find out.

In a hushed voice I said, "Billy, we're going to calmly stand up now and get out of here, follow me."

I tried to walk as casually as I could considering the circum-stances. Billy followed beside me. When we got about halfway to the second door, the men standing at the entryway charged at us and rammed into us hard, throwing Billy and me into the bar. Then the three dudes at the table decided to jump up and lend a hand.

We fought back, but they managed to subdue us pretty quickly, partly due to the fact that we were exhausted and outnumbered. The six men held us to the ground, kicked us in our ribs, stomach, chest, and backs, while the bartender and other dude used chicken wire to bind our wrists behind our backs and to our ankles. It cut deep into our skin and I lost sensation in my hands immediately.

Next, they carried us out the front door and threw us into the back of a pickup truck. The metal on the bed of the truck was so hot that it burned our backs and legs. Angry people crowded around, yelling curses, punching and spitting at us. It was a wild, chaotic scene to say the least.

The truck spun out and took off at high speed. Racing down the road I noticed that we bounced past several rebel checkpoints en route to wherever it was we were going. My skin was on fire and the pain from the wire around my wrists was so excruciating that I was sure I would lose my hands.

An hour or so later, the truck stopped in front of a little building and a man in a uniform came out. Another group of men carried us inside of what turned out to be a run-down jail. They threw us into a tiny cell and slammed the door shut behind us. Our teammate Greg was already there, badly beaten and looking scared to death.

The cell contained bunks made out of plywood, but no mattresses, and a hole in the floor covered with dead flies. In the corner was a metal can with a black, oily, thick liquid in it with a metal ladle.

A six-foot-tall transvestite guard came into our cell and scooped up some of the black fluids. The guard dipped a ladle into the bucket and held it up to the bars. Boys and men pushed their mouths and tongues to the edge of the cell, desperately trying to lap up even a small bit of the liquid. There was a lot of pushing and shoving as they tried to jockey their way into position, just for a taste of that disgusting looking substance.

That guard resembled a character from a bad movie, with poorly applied lipstick and mascara, a strange leer on her face, and covered in filth from head to toe. After dispensing several ladles full to the guys in the opposite cell, s/he walked over to us and grinned. Flies buzzed around the bucket. S/he offered us a ladle filled with the liquid as well. Even through the three of us were extremely thirsty and hungry, there was no way we were going to drink that shit. Whatever was in that bucket couldn't have been good for us.

"No thanks," I said through parched lips.

Later, as we sat there in the cell, two guards approached with a set of wire cutters. With great difficulty, they were able to snap the chicken wire off our wrists and ankles. By that time, our hands and feet were completely numb, purple, and swollen. It took a long time for the circulation to return, but we were happy to be free from the wires.

Greg, who was convinced that we were going to be executed, started to weep openly. Billy got down on his knees and began to pray. I dropped and did pushups and then walked over to the bunk and did sets of dips. They looked at me like I was crazy, but we each had our own coping mechanisms.

I kept telling myself that there had to be a way out. We just had to find it. Turning to the other guys, I said, "We'll be fine. Don't worry."

"Really, Don?" they asked incredulously.

"Yes!"

The transvestite guard offered the liquid to us one more time. "*Bebe.*"

I shook my head, "no." S/he shrugged and shuffled off back down the hall.

Greg got angry. Glaring at me, he said, "What the hell did you do that for?"

"Because if we drink that shit we'll get sick," I answered.

"Great. So we'll die of dehydration instead," he shot back.

"No, we won't," I answered, trying to muster up as much confidence in my voice as I could.

I knew I had to stay positive, be smart and do everything possible to get us out of there. I summoned up all the lessons I'd learned from my training and the mental toughness I'd developed as a SEAL.

I reminded myself that I'd gotten out of many tight scrapes in the past, and would get out of this one too. Quitting wasn't an option, and there was no point thinking about the bad things that could happen. I had to focus on the here and now and figure out what I could do to help our situation.

For the next two days and nights, I barely slept. Instead, I worked out and spoke to the six or so guards every chance I got. In my rudimentary Spanish, I tried to engage them in conversation about anything I could think of, including the excessive heat, our need for clean water, and the local senoritas. Most of them just continued to be overly hostile and expressed their hatred of all gringos.

But I did manage to develop a kind of relationship with two of them: a skinny nineteen-year-old named Paco who had a big scar on his face from being kicked by a horse, and an older farmer named Ramon. They worked the late shift from midnight to eight in the morning, which made it easy to engage them in conversation.

Ramon mostly listened while Paco did the majority of the talking. He was in love with his young wife Celia and they were expecting a child. In the early morning hours of the second day, he showed me a photograph of Celia. I told him that I was so dizzy from the lack of water that my eyes couldn't focus. He muttered something to Ramon who came back with a bucket filled with clean water and a little plastic cup.

I woke Greg and Billy. As we took turns gulping the water down, Paco said that he and Ramon didn't hate Americans like some of their compatriots. They were fighting, he said, for a better life for their friends and families.

I nodded and said, "*Yo comprendo,*" indicating that I understood.

While everyone else slept around us, I told him that holding me and my colleagues wouldn't help them realize their goal, because the people I worked for were cold-blooded killers. If anything happened to us they'd seek revenge, hunting down all the guards and killing their wives and children. They'd probably bomb the entire village to the ground. I said that I disagreed with his political agenda but admired his courage.

Paco told me that he was prepared to die. But as he said it, I detected a profound sadness in his eyes. He may have been ready to sacrifice himself for the cause, but that didn't mean he wanted to see his wife and unborn child get caught up in the fight too.

That morning, the transvestite guard smashed me in the face with a long wooden pole for no apparent reason and then just walked away. It was a sharp reminder that we had to find some way to get out of there, and soon. I spent the rest of the day working out while looking for a way to escape. When Paco and Ramon assumed guard duty at midnight, they refused to talk.

In the wee hours of the morning, the two of them and another guard roughly woke the three of us from our slumber. Without saying a word, they bound our wrists and ankles with chicken wire again, and dragged us back to the same pickup that had been used to deliver us to the jail several days earlier.

"They're going to kill us and dump our bodies," Greg groaned as we bounced along on rough dirt roads at a high rate of speed.

"No, they won't," I promised, perhaps even trying to convince myself.

"This is your fault for pissing off the guards."

The sun rose behind us. Even in my weakened state, I tried to stay positive. I said to myself, "I'm not going to die. Not today and not like this."

After driving for about forty minutes, the truck skidded to a halt in the middle of a field near a dry riverbed. The guards jumped out of the cab, pulled us out of the truck, and roughly dropped us onto the ground. They took our shoes, shirts and socks, and drove off in a cloud of dust.

We lay on the ground in our underwear with no compass, no means of communicating with our base, no tools, no weapons, and the air around us growing hotter by the minute.

"This is worse than getting shot," Greg complained as we dragged ourselves out of the direct sunlight.

Billy agreed. "Yeah, now we starve to death and get eaten by vultures."

"Guys," I said. "There's no point thinking like that. We are alive and free!"

Even though I was starting to feel delirious from the lack of food and water, I recalled the training I had received from the SERE (Navy Survival, Evasion, Resistance, and Escape) course I had taken a couple years earlier. I showed my buddies how to use a rock to slowly grind through the wire that bound our feet. It took some time and effort, but we were able to free our ankles and wrists, which allowed us to stand.

"Now what do we do?" Greg asked.

"We walk," I told him.

"Where?" he asked desperately.

"Downstream," I said, already starting to walk in that direction.

"But the river is completely dry."

"Follow me."

I led the way in bare feet down the dried riverbed, with my two teammates close behind. As the sun rose in the sky the temperature climbed as well, and soon there were buzzards circling overhead. Although Greg wanted to stop, I insisted that we keep walking and remain vigilant to possible enemy personnel. I was also keeping an eye out for sources of water, especially man-made ones like wells, tanks, pumps, or irrigation canals.

An hour or so later, we stumbled into a grove of cassava trees, taking refuge in the first shade we'd seen in hours. I figured that if the trees could stay green and grow, there had to be a source of water nearby. While Greg and Billy rested out of the sun, I found an irrigation ditch and followed it to a spigot. When I opened it fresh, clear water came rushing out.

Feeling like I had won a million bucks, I ran back and told Billy and Greg about the water, but not before taking a few big gulps and dipping my head under the cool stream. It felt amazing.

"You sure you aren't hallucinating?" Greg asked when I told them about my find.

All I had to do is point at my wet t-shirt and hair and his and Billy's eyes lit up.

Again I said, "Follow me."

As they drank and washed their faces, I spotted a farmer and his son in a field nearby. I approached them cautiously and using my limited Spanish vocabulary, I explained that my two friends and I were foreigners who had gotten lost and that there was a big reward for them if they could point me in a direction where I could call for help.

In exchange for the promise of money, the boy led me to a nearby village where I found a phone and called my command. After night-fall a helicopter landed nearby. I handed the farmer a fistful of dollars I received from the co-pilot and thanked him profusely. A few minutes later we were in the air and on our way home.

My relief was enormous. As we ascended into the night sky, I remember thinking that I had learned something important between BUD/S and my time with the SEAL Teams. I had learned that whatever the challenge, the worst thing you can do is quit. Because few problems are truly insurmountable, and if you just mange to hang in there you'll either find a solution or one will present itself.

Decades of combat and life experience later, I believe that even more strongly. Simple perseverance is the first key to success. Almost every successful person has encountered opposition at some point. But they don't let it stop them. In fact, they use that adversity to fuel their ambitions and look for ways to overcome all obstacles. The bottom line is, whatever you're trying to achieve, my first piece of advice is: don't quit!

ERNEST SHACKLETON
Polar Explorer

One of the greatest examples of man learning to push beyond his boundaries is that of Ernest Shackleton and the crew of his ship *The Endurance*. Few humans have ever had to contend with such trying circumstances and grueling conditions during which their physical and mental limits were tested for months on end. Their story is one of hardship and difficulty, but also incredible inspiration too. It also happens to quite possibly be the greatest survival story ever.

In the early years of the twentieth century, Ernest Shackleton was an Irish polar explorer caught up in the race to become the first person to reach the South Pole. He had embarked on several expeditions to the Antarctic and was determined to plant the British flag at the bottom of the world. Unfortunately for him however, he was beaten to the punch by Norwegian Roald Amundsen, who arrived at the Pole in December of 1911, approximately twenty-five days before another British explorer named Robert Falcon Scott.

Undaunted by this setback, Shackleton was still determined to play a major role in mapping out the Antarctic continent. He came up with the idea of becoming the first person to traverse that remote and inhospitable place, which would be an even bigger feat than reaching the South Pole. With that plan in mind, in August of 1914 he sailed out of London on a ship called *Endurance*.

At the time, World War I was just breaking out in Europe, but no one thought the conflict would last for very long, nor that the explorer and his men would be needed for the fight. In fact when Shackleton inquired as to whether or not he and the crew should delay their voyage, they received a telegram from the First Lord of the Admiralty Winston Churchill himself regarding the matter. That message contained just one word with Churchill instructing Shackleton to "proceed."

Shackleton knew that his expedition across Antarctica would be his most ambitious polar journey yet. The traverse would cover more than a thousand miles of completely unexplored and untamed wilderness covered in snow and ice. The plan was to use sled dogs as Amundsen had done on his journey to the Pole, which would help Shackleton and his men to move at a much faster pace, ensuring that the expedition would be over before the return of the austral winter.

Unfortunately, Shackleton and the crew of the *Endurance* never even made it to their starting point along the Antarctic coast. On January 19, 1915 the ship became stuck in the pack ice that surrounds the continent, making it impossible to continue forward or turn back. Despite their best efforts, there was no way to free the vessel from the icy grip that Mother Nature had placed on her. The only answer was to wait until the arrival of spring, when warmer temperatures would free the ship at last.

And wait they did, stranded in the coldest conditions imaginable, until spring arrived late in 1915. For ten long months they had been locked in place, doing their best to survive in one of the most inhospitable environments on the planet. But when the ice finally started to break up at long last, it also began to put enormous pressure on the *Endurance*, eventually cracking its hull and sending the vessel to the bottom of the ocean.

Before that happened however, Shackleton had the foresight to order his crew to abandon ship and set up camp on the ice. That happened in October and they would remain encamped there for two more months, hoping beyond hope that another ship would come looking for them. When that didn't happen, they decided to strike out for the nearest island in the lifeboats that had been salvaged from the *Endurance* before it sank. Braving frigid waters and ferocious winds, the crew made its way across open water to reach a place called Elephant Island, a desolate rock in the middle of the Southern Ocean that was far off the beaten path of the regular shipping routes.

Knowing that a rescue ship was unlikely to find them at that remote location, Shackleton decided to hatch a desperate plan. Winter was fast approaching and the crew was getting increasingly short on food and supplies. He came up with the idea of modifying one of the lifeboats to make an open ocean crossing. His plan was to set out for South Georgia Island to seek aid from one of the whaling stations that operated there. It was an all-or-nothing venture that would either result in success or death.

Once the preparations were complete, Shackleton and five of his men set out across the Southern Ocean, battling massive waves, high winds, and storms while en route. Navigating by dead reckoning, they spent fifteen days at sea, finally arriving at their destination completely exhausted, starving, and at the end of their rope. Unfortunately, they arrived on the wrong side of the island, far from any of the whaling stations that could actually provide assistance.

In order to reach one of the inhabited villages on the far side of the island, the men would have to trek across the interior of South Georgia, a rugged, mountainous place that was mostly unexplored at that time. Three of the crew had taken ill while at sea, which left just Shackleton and two others to make the trek. They traveled through some of the most difficult and demanding terrain imaginable, covering an unbelievable thirty-two miles in thirty-six hours in order to reach a whaling station where they could find help.

To put Shackleton's trek into perspective, modern explorers have attempted to replicate the feat, crossing the island along the same remote route. Most haven't been able to complete the route at the same pace, even using modern gear and equipment. Perhaps even more impressive is that fact that Shackleton and his men did the hike after being stranded in the Antarctic for nearly sixteen months. After that much time in the wild, they were completely unrecognizable upon arriving at the whaling station.

Shackleton immediately went to work organizing a rescue for his men who were still stranded on Elephant Island. A ship was dispatched to rescue the crew, but due to thick ice and terrible weather it was unable to approach the remote isle on its first attempt. It would take another three months before an icebreaker could make its way through. When it did, Shackleton stood boldly on the bow, calling to his crew to let them know that help had arrived at long last.

All told, the crew of the *Endurance* were stranded in the Antarctic for more than eighteen months, facing untold hardships that ranged from exposure to extreme weather conditions to frostbite to malnutrition. But through it all, they stayed focused, committed, and loyal to Shackleton and as a result, not a single man died during the ill-fated expedition. That remarkable fact has always stuck with me, a reminder of what the human spirit is capable of achieving, even under extreme duress.

The polar explorer and all twenty-two of his men returned home safely only to discover that the conflict on the European continent had not ended as quickly as predicted. In fact, it had flared up into the most devastating war that the human race had ever seen. As a result, Shackleton and his men were soon pressed into service, with many of them shipping out to the Eastern Front. They had survived the demanding conditions of the Antarctic only to be met with the meat-grinder that was World War I. It was out of the frying pan and into the fire for the men of the *Endurance*, who had already suffered more than most humans could ever imagine.

There is so much that we can learn from Shackleton and his

crew that it is hard to know even where to begin. Not only did each and every one of them possess a tough mindset, they were also able to push beyond their normal boundaries simply because there was no other choice. They either had to find ways to adapt, improvise, and overcome all of the obstacles put in their way, or they weren't going to survive. Given those choices, all they could do was continue to look for ways to give themselves a chance to make it through another day. It wasn't easy. They had to endure some horrific conditions and make hard choices in order to survive, but they did it anyway. The crew of the *Endurance* showed remarkable resolve in the face of nearly impossible odds.

And Shackleton himself was the glue that held them all together. It was his decision making, goal setting, and unflappable demeanor that gave the rest of the men hope. If "the boss" thought there was a chance they could make it home, the rest of them weren't about to give up hope either. They believed completely in his leadership and experience, and in the end he repaid that loyalty back by making sure that everyone returned home to their friends and family.

Throughout the eighteen-month ordeal Shackleton and his crew learned exactly where their boundaries were defined. They learned that they could push through almost any challenge and come out the other side stronger than they were before. Mother Nature threw everything she had at them, and yet they still survived.

Considering the extremely long odds that they faced, it is hard to not be inspired by the story of the *Endurance* and her crew. The challenges that they faced on their journey make some of the daily obstacles the rest of us face seem paltry and insignificant in comparison. Think about that the next time you want to throw in the towel while trying to achieve whatever it is you want to accomplish. Chances are it isn't even remotely close to what Shackleton and his men had to face.

Chapter 3

SETTING MICRO-GOALS AND MACRO-GOALS

"Impossible is just a word thrown around by small men who find it easier to live in the world they've been given than to explore the power they have to change it."

—Muhammad Ali

In 1995 while competing at the Ironman World Championship in Kona, Hawaii, American triathlete Mark Allen found himself in an unusual position. As he entered the transition area that marked the end of the cycling stage and the start of the marathon-distance run, he learned that he was more than thirteen minutes behind German Thomas Hellriegel who had just put in a dominant performance on the bike. In the world of competitive endurance sports, that is a nearly insurmountable lead, even for a guy who had won at Kona on five previous occasions.

Not one to ever give up, Allen quickly switched out of his cycling gear and into his running shoes to start the final stage of the race. At the time, the thought of making up thirteen minutes on a tough competitor like Hellriegel was simply too overwhelming to consider, particularly after already completing two very difficult stages just to get to that point in the race.

A traditional Olympic-distance triathlon includes a .9-mile swim, a 24.8-mile bike ride, and a 6.2-mile run. But an Ironman ups the difficulty considerably, stretching those distances out to a 2.4-mile swim, a 112-mile ride, and a 26.2-mile run (a full marathon), turning the race into what many believe is the toughest single-day sporting event in the world.

As if those lengths weren't already daunting enough, the course at Kona is legendary for its ability to punish athletes. Some athletes come to compete in what they think will be an island paradise, only to discover blistering heat, high winds, and a surprising amount of vertical gain and loss along the route. As a result, even the toughest competitors can be crushed under the physical and mental demands that come along with this brutally difficult race.

As Allen left the final transition area that day he wasn't thinking about how he could erase Hellriegel's thirteen-minute lead. Instead, he was focused on a much smaller scale. He thought that if he could just make up a single inch with each stride, he might be able to claw his way back into contention. Just one inch with every step could be the difference between going home an Ironman champ for a sixth time or finishing as an also-ran.

It wasn't going to be easy. In addition to trying to play catch-up with a supreme athlete like Hellriegel, Kona's notorious weather conditions were out in full force. Not only had the mercury climbed well above 100°F, but ferocious winds buffeted the competitors all day long. In fact, at the time they were the fiercest winds that anyone had ever seen at the World Championships, making it difficult to ride and run, and completely sapping the energy from the legs of the competitors.

An hour into the marathon stage it was clear that Allen was the stronger of the two runners. He moved smoothly and easily, while Hellriegel began to labor. The German still held a sizable lead, but the American was gaining. The question was, would Hellriegel be able to hang on or would Allen be able to catch him before the finish line.

At the 23.5-mile mark, the two men finally met out on the course as Allen caught the German at long last. But, with just a little more than two miles to go, Hellriegel wasn't ready to concede defeat. He raced stride for stride with the American for as long as he could, before eventually fading down the stretch.

In the end, Allen would finish more than two minutes ahead of his rival and claim yet another Ironman World Championship in the process. His performance that day would lead to one of the most improbable comebacks in the history of the sport and stands as a testament to his mental toughness and determination. It is also a perfect example of setting micro-goals to achieve macro-goals.

What can we learn from Mark Allen's performance in that race? For starters, it is a classic case of never giving up until you've achieved your goal. In this case, that goal wasn't just to finish one of the toughest sporting events in the world, but to win it too. When he was trailing by thirteen minutes and facing grueling weather conditions, that seemed all-but impossible to do. But by realistically assessing the challenge that he faced, then breaking it down into easy to understand numbers, Allen was able to begin the arduous task of closing the gap.

When Allen set off on his twenty-six-mile run, he wasn't thinking about the massive lead that Hellriegel held on him or how exactly he was going to overcome the thirteen-minute gap the German had opened. Instead, he focused solely on trying to make up a single inch with each stride, pushing himself to go just a little bit faster as a result. A single inch isn't much in the grand scheme of things, but a lot of inches can add up quickly, especially over the length of a marathon. When the dust finally settled, he ended up completing the run in two hours, forty-two minutes, and eight seconds. That's not too bad considering he had already finished a 2.4 mile swim and ridden his bike for 112 miles.

Allen once said that "A man must not withdraw from the sport, without having given at least once in a lifetime all that he had." As an Ironman legend, you can bet that Mark always gave everything that he had when competing in a race. That's how you become a six-time champion and an absolute legend amongst endurance athletes.

The idea of setting micro-goals to achieve macro-goals is an important part of learning to push beyond our own boundaries. In fact, those micro-goals are the initial steps that start us along the path towards getting to wherever it is we want to go. Identifying what those smaller goals are also helps us to formulate a plan. In a sense, they are the building blocks towards achievement.

I first realized the importance of setting micro- and macro-goals when I was a teenager. At the time, I had one foot in the grave and the other on slick ice, constantly getting into scrapes with the law and lacking any kind of direction whatsoever. I was headed nowhere fast and my prospects for the future weren't great.

I didn't know it at the time, but that all changed the day I went for that fateful run with my friend Dave Kelleher. I was so proud that I was running with my good friend and hero. He was a champion and I wanted to be a champion just like him. We both were approximately the same age, body weight, height etc., but he was a pro and I was just a novice, and I knew that if I trained like him, I'd become a better rider.

After our first lap, I was feeling really uncomfortable, I did not enjoy running at all and I hoped that somehow the other laps were not going to be quite as miserable. After all, I was a non-runner and had no idea what I was getting myself into. Mile two was worse, and that was followed by mile three, which was when I simply gave up. I was too uncomfortable and too tired to continue. I felt bad for myself and I quit just three miles in.

I watched Dave run, lap after lap, each mile he looked more uncomfortable, but he was focused and was pushing himself. That was when I discovered the difference between someone who just settles for where they are in life and someone who is successful. He pushed himself hard and did not lose focus. When things got tough and I was out of my element, I looked for an easy way out.

After that miserable performance, Dave told me that if I wanted to get serious about being a pro motocross rider, I needed to start training and get myself into better shape. He recommended I take up running a few times a week and maybe even train for a running race.

At the time, I wasn't even aware that there were running races. My first thought, was *how boring—a running race. That doesn't seem nearly as exciting as riding a motorcycle.*

I asked Dave when the next race was. He told me, somewhat jokingly, that the Boston Marathon was just a few months away.

"Boston Marathon?" I asked. "How long is that?"

"It's 26.2 miles," Dave answered.

I looked at him incredulously. "26.2 miles? No one runs that far."

Dave assured me that there were thousands of people who could do just that, with many of them competing in marathons all over the country. He recommended I pick up a copy of *The Complete Book of Running* (1977) by Jim Fixx to help broaden my knowledge on the subject.

It wasn't long before I managed to track down a copy and started to absorb everything I could from it. I read about the Boston Marathon, which was the same race that Dave had mentioned to me. I also read about all kinds of interesting people who run long distances, including young people, old people, and handicapped people. It seems that people from pretty much all walks of life liked to run and competed in a variety of races on a regular basis. I asked myself, *if they could do it, why couldn't I?*

It was about then that I set a macro-goal of finishing the Boston Marathon that year without stopping to walk or take a break. In order to get that point with my conditioning, I knew that I would have to start training and competing in other races first. I set micro-goals of running 5Ks, 10Ks, and 10-mile races, each at a faster pace. In this way, I slowly went from a guy who quit after jogging just three miles, to someone who was easily able to cover that distance—and a lot farther—at a respectable pace.

Finishing Boston hurt a lot but I didn't stop once along the way and managed to cross the finish line with a time of 3:44. It was a solid effort for my first full marathon, but I knew I could do better. This led directly to my next macro-goal, which was to run my next marathon at an even faster pace. With the focus of my training shifting towards speed, I was able to shave significant time off my pace, and within three years I was able to get my time down to 2:49.

Having conquered the marathon, my micro- and macro-goals shifted once again. Now, running a twenty-six-mile race was no longer challenging enough, reducing it to micro-goal status. In its place, I turned my attention to running fifty-mile and 100K ultramarathons instead, making that my macro objective. And when that was achieved I moved onto a new macro-goal of competing in Ironman triathlons, double-Ironman races, and multi-day adventure races, too.

My new goal-setting philosophy was working extremely well and I was achieving things I never thought possible. My confidence level was soaring, and it got to the point that if I didn't claim a podium spot (finishing first, second, or third), I was disappointed in my effort. Setting smaller, more achievable goals, was proving to be the stepping stones I needed to get to my larger ones. The formula was simple, yet effective. All I knew was that I couldn't lose focus on that macro-goal if I actually wanted to achieve it.

When first developing this process I quickly realized that our micro-goals need to be achievable and they should naturally build into the macro-goals we've set for ourselves. In this way, we're constantly making progress towards whatever it is we want to achieve, and the skills and conditioning that we pick up along the way are useful for helping us to get there.

How does this work exactly? Let's say that you're a beginning runner and your macro-goal is to eventually run a marathon. At first, that will sound incredibly daunting, especially when jogging just a couple of miles seems really painful and difficult. But by setting a micro-goal of running two miles every day for several days in row, you've given yourself a challenge that is tough, but not unobtainable.

When you first begin training you'll feel slow, ponderous, and even uncomfortable at times. Your legs will be sore, your lungs will gasp for air, and you'll probably be asking yourself why you ever took up running in the first place. There will almost certainly be times when you'll want to quit. But if you refuse to give in, stay consistent with your training, and push through those moments when you just want to stop, you will become stronger and faster.

Before long, you'll be able to comfortably run those two miles without stopping. Your body will grow accustomed to the workouts and that distance won't seem all that far any longer. It is then that you'll want to set a new micro-goal of running three or four miles instead. The point is to make sure that the new goal remains a challenge, yet one that is still within your reach. And when that goal has been attained, raise the bar even higher, covering the same distance at a faster pace or pushing yourself to run longer distances as you inch your way towards that marathon.

You don't have to be a runner to see the value of this process, as it can be used to achieve just about anything in life. Whether you're looking to climb a mountain, become a better student, launch some personal project, or succeed in business, identifying your ultimate goal and visualizing the steps you need to get there, is one of the keys to success. Here, I'm simply using sports as an analogy for other areas of your life, but the concept remains the same no matter where you apply it.

Elon Musk, the billionaire founder of Tesla Motors, understands the concept of setting micro-goals to achieve macro-goals. He has done it a number of times throughout his illustrious career and has achieved great success along the way. He has even managed to pull off something that others once thought completely impossible—creating a privately owned space program.

In 2001, Musk came up with an idea that he hoped would simultaneously reinvigorate the public's interest in space travel and boost NASA's budget. America's venerable space program continued to see a steady stream of funding over the years, but thanks to inflation and a full slate of expensive projects, the space agency hasn't been able to introduce any concrete plans to send manned spacecraft beyond Earth's orbit.

The charismatic Musk has said on more than one occasion that the biggest disappointment of his life would be dying before humans have a chance to land on Mars. So, he took it upon himself to create a pet-project that would involve sending a miniature greenhouse to the red planet as proof that life can survive there.

In order to get this project off the ground, Musk traveled to Russia to buy a rocket that could take his payload into space. Unfortunately, he couldn't obtain one at a price he was willing to pay, so he returned home empty-handed. But on the flight back to the US, Musk had a revelation that would eventually lead to him creating his own rockets and revolutionize our concept of space travel.

Musk realized that the raw materials used to create a rocket made up just a fraction of the total asking price to buy one that was already assembled. This prompted him to stop shopping for a rocket and start thinking about building one himself. By bringing the design and testing in-house, and using a modular approach to development that he had learned while creating software, he calculated that he could cut the cost of launching a rocket dramatically while potentially pocketing a healthy profit at the same time. It was from that revelation that SpaceX was born.

But even Elon Musk doesn't just go to work one day and decide that he is going to start sending rockets into space. There was a lot of work that needed to be done before that could ever happen. He started by first identifying his macro-goal—creating a financially viable private space program—and began working on the micro-goals that would eventually allow him to get there.

That meant starting small by first building a launch vehicle that wasn't especially powerful or complex, but still delivered a level of performance that could meet the demands of potential customers. The plan was to make incremental steps towards creating a new rocket before scaling up to larger projects with bigger ambitions. This helped to not only maximize SpaceX's chances for success, but also limited the potential for a disastrous setback that could ruin the fledgling company before it ever got off the ground.

Musk assembled a team of engineers and scientists to help him reach these goals and in the ensuing years they designed, built, and tested propulsion and guidance systems, maneuvering thrusters, capsules for carrying cargo, and much more. There were literally thousands of small steps that needed to be taken before they could even begin their first tests of the new rocket, which was dubbed the Falcon 1. Some were monumental, others were fairly minor, all were crucial.

All of the high-tech components that made up the Falcon 1 were first heavily tested on the ground to ensure that they would work properly and meet the standards needed to perform in space. It was, at times, a painstakingly slow and deliberate process that eventually culminated with the first ever privately-funded rocket reaching Earth orbit in 2008.

Of course, there were more than few setbacks along the way. Two years prior to its first successful launch, SpaceX's original Falcon 1 rocket exploded spectacularly just thirty-three seconds into flight. In 2007 the second attempt failed to reach orbit, crashing unceremoniously into the ocean. A year later another high-profile mission ended prematurely when two stages of the rocket collided with one another after separation, sending the cargo capsule spinning out of control before it too eventually crashed back to Earth.

Through it all, Musk remained committed to the project however and persistently soldiered on, even when it looked like the entire company could come crashing down around him. Along the way, he continually learned from his mistakes and took each setback in stride. No one ever said building your own space program from the ground up would be easy, and yet the SpaceX team continually found creative solutions to problems and eventually brought it all together.

Today, SpaceX is a true success story. Musk's company has gone on to create a reusable rocket system called the Falcon 9 that is capable of making regular flights into orbit, landing safely back on the ground, and being prepped for relaunch again within a matter of days. This was all engineered at a fraction of the cost it would have taken NASA to develop the same orbital system and has resulted in the company winning a number of lucrative government and private contracts for delivering supplies to the International Space Station and launching satellites into orbit. All of that was accomplished by staying focused, remaining persistent, and continually identifying the next micro-goal that would continue the company along the trajectory that its founder had set for it.

Not one to rest on his laurels, Musk isn't done just yet. Now that he has built an efficient, cost-effective space program, he has returned to the project that started him down this path in the first place—sending humans to Mars. The ambitious entrepreneur has created a roadmap for colonizing the red planet, something he thinks can be accomplished within the next decade.

Conquering our micro-goals also brings some additional benefits that aren't always noticeable at first. For instance, by giving us a series of achievable objectives we also start to build self-confidence, too. It is not unusual to have a bit of trepidation when setting out in pursuit of a larger goal, as we're not always sure of the best way to proceed when trying to get there. But as we make progress along the way, our confidence naturally builds too, erasing much of the doubt and uncertainty we felt at the beginning.

Using our earlier analogy of the beginning runner looking to finish his or her first marathon, it is easy to see how confidence can play a key role in preparing for such an event. At the beginning, the idea of running a mile or two without stopping comes with a lot of uncertainty, particularly if you've never done it before. But after training hard, consistently hitting weekly distance goals, and getting stronger physically and mentally, those few miles will soon be a piece of cake.

In my own experience, I went from being a total non-runner to finishing my first marathon in a matter of just a few months. Getting that race under my belt was a big confidence booster, bestowing on me the knowledge that I could run the entire 26.2 mile distance without stopping or wanting to quit. This allowed me to concentrate on my next goal, which was to lower my overall time in subsequent races.

Eventually I'd go on to compete in more than thirty marathons or ultramarathons over the course of three years, which is a hectic pace for those kinds of distances. But the confidence I gained from competing in those events allowed me to not just get faster, but to branch out into other sports, as well. But like everyone else, I was just a beginning runner once myself. If I can do it, so can you.

Chinese philosopher Lao Tzu famously remarked in his *Tao Te Ching* that "a journey of a thousand miles begins with a single step." That sums up the idea of using micro-goals to achieve larger objectives incredibly well. No matter what personal journey you happen to be on, you'll have to start with that first step. And while at times, the finish line may seem like it is impossibly out of reach, if you just focus on putting one foot in front of the other, you'll slowly and steadily make progress towards the destination, whatever that destination happens to be.

This approach can be used in just about every aspect of your life, from running errands and completing a to-do list, all the way up to plotting world domination. Sometimes, it can even be a matter of survival. This is something that mountaineer Joe Simpson learned all too well while climbing Siula Grande, a 20,813-foot peak located in the Peruvian Andes of South America.

Simpson's story is well-known for anyone who has read his book, *Touching the Void* (1988), or caught the 2003 documentary film of the same name. In 1985, Simpson and his climbing partner, Simon Yates, traveled to Peru to take on the previously unclimbed West Face of Siula Grande. It was a difficult and demanding ascent, but after several days of climbing the two men managed to reach the summit and were ecstatic over their accomplishment.

But on the descent, their joy quickly turned to horror. Simpson slipped over the edge of an icy cliff, and landed hard on the frozen ground below, shattering his tibia while simultaneously pushing the bone upward into his knee joint. This rendered his right leg completely useless. The injury was horribly painful, making it excruciating for Simpson to stand, let alone attempt to walk down a mountain.

To make matters worse, the climb to the summit took longer than expected and as a result he and Yates were running low on supplies. Bad weather was also starting to move in, which is always a recipe for disaster in the mountains. Descending another three thousand feet to reach their base camp was going to be a challenge under the best of circumstances, now it had become a daunting task that could put the lives of both men in jeopardy.

Unwilling to leave his friend behind, Yates tied two 150-foot ropes together, than fastened one end to Simpson. The plan was to lower him down the mountain three hundred feet at a time until they could reach safety. At the midway point of each of those three-hundred-foot sections, Simpson would have to stand on his left leg momentarily to provide some slack for Yates, who would then pass the knot uniting the two ropes through a belay plate, which is a safety device that helps control a climber's descent.

Using this approach, the two men continued to make their way down the mountain, with Simpson in considerably pain, but grateful to have not been abandoned altogether. Whenever he would reach the end of a three-hundred-foot segment, he would give it a tug to signal to Yates that it was his turn to descend. The system worked reasonably well, although it was taking a very long time to descend. Still, at least they were making progress towards their goal, which was to reach their camp and try to find help for the injured climber.

Eventually, darkness descended on the mountain and poor weather conditions closed in, too. It was becoming harder and harder for Yates to spot his partner at the end of the rope and with the wind howling, it had become just about impossible to communicate verbally. At one point, Yates accidentally lowered Simpson over the edge of a cliff, and the injured climber found himself dangling helplessly in empty space. Unable to climb up or signal to his friend, all he could do was wait and hope for the best.

For his part, Yates held onto the rope for as long as he could. Unsure of what was happening below him, he continued to wait for a signal from Simpson to let him know everything was alright. After sitting there for what felt like hours, it began to dawn on him that something had gone terribly wrong. Yates wasn't sure what had happened to his friend, but he knew that he couldn't pull him back up the mountain nor could he continue down while still tied to the rope. Worse yet, the seat he had dug into the snow had begun to give way and Yates knew that soon he would be pulled down the side of the mountain along with Simpson. Given no other choice, he elected to cut the rope, sending his friend tumbling into the abyss.

Heartbroken, Yates dug a snow cave and waited out the storm. The following day, he resumed his trek down the slope, completely convinced that his friend had perished in the fall the night before. When he reached their camp, he was exhausted and inconsolable with grief. Crawling inside his sleeping bag, he slipped into a fitful sleep, wrestling with his own demons as a voice inside his head continually asked if he had done the right thing.

But Simpson did not die in the fall. Instead, he tumbled 150-feet into a deep crevasse, coming to rest on a small ledge, where he immediately passed out from pain and exhaustion. When he came to, he realized his predicament. Alone, injured, and undoubtedly left for dead, he knew he had to get off the mountain if he wanted to survive.

To do that, he began to make a plan, which involved breaking down the challenge ahead of him into smaller, more achievable sections. First and foremost, he had to get himself out of the crevasse, but unable to climb upwards, he had no other choice but to descend deeper into the ice in search of an alternate exit.

Fortunately he found one, although it was located at the top of a steep snow slope. To get out, he would have to crawl up that slope, using his arms and one good leg to propel him along. Eventually he reached the exit and found himself back on the slopes of Siula Grande, still a very long way from help, although progress had been made.

Escaping the crevasse was a major milestone, but it was just the start of Simpson's ordeal. Over the following three days, he would crawl on his hands and knees, or hop along on one leg, often using an ice axe as a makeshift crutch. With almost no food or water, he eventually managed to cover more than five miles before deliriously wandering into camp where he found Yates preparing to pack up and depart for home. Had he been even a little later, chances are his climbing partner would have been gone, leaving him on the mountain completely alone.

Joe Simpson's harrowing descent of Siula Grande is one of the greatest survival stories in mountaineering history. It is also the perfect example of how a tough mindset and setting of micro-goals can help you get through almost anything. At the time, the thought of crawling all the way back to his campsite was almost too overwhelming for Simpson to comprehend. So instead, he would set smaller objectives in his mind. For example, he might spot a rock or shrub in the distance and tell himself to just reach that spot. *Get there, and you can rest*, he'd tell himself. Once that goal was achieved, he'd catch his breath, regain his strength, spot another landmark, and push himself onward to that place too.

This process went on for what must have seemed like forever, and as the hours crawled by it took every ounce of strength and energy to continue. But in the end, he successfully got down from the mountain. Simpson would spend weeks in a Peruvian hospital and faced months of torturous rehab, but eventually he would not only walk again, but would return to climbing, having a long and distinguished mountaineering career.

It took a very different kind of traumatic experience for comedian and actor Tim Allen to learn the benefits of setting and chasing goals, but it was definitely a lesson well learned. In 1978, Allen was arrested at an airport in Michigan for possession of 650 grams of cocaine. At the time, that was enough to earn him a life sentence in prison, but he managed to make a plea deal and was ordered to serve three to seven years instead.

Allen has said that his time in jail was a watershed moment in his life that forced him to take a look at what he was doing and refocus on the things that mattered the most. He made amends to his friends and family, then turned his attention towards creating a more productive future for himself. This change in attitude came—at least in part—from reading motivational books while he served his sentence. Those books helped to convince him that he could accomplish big things if he just set his mind to it.

After serving two years and four months of his sentence, Allen was released from prison and soon adopted his own form of setting micro-goals to achieve long-term objectives. He decided to write down the things that he hoped to achieve, but he had a unique approach to doing so. He separated those goals into three categories: the things he wanted to achieve that day, the things he wanted to do that year, and the goals he had for himself over the course of his life. In doing so, he was reminding himself of the things that he wanted to get done immediately, while never losing sight of where he wanted to go with his life in the next year, and beyond.

Prior to going to prison, Allen had started doing stand-up comedy, but hadn't really seriously thought about making it his career. After being released on parole, it became a real goal for him, and not long after he moved to Los Angeles and began pursuing that dream. Before long, he was a regular at some of the local comedy clubs, earning himself a reputation for being hardworking and talented, a rare combination in Hollywood. Eventually he would hit it big with his stand-up specials followed by the television show *Home Improvement*. The rest is history.

Despite being a major success in both television and movies, Allen still adheres to the same goal-setting strategy that he adopted after getting out of prison. Every morning he continues to write down his objectives for the day, the year, and his life. This idea of setting micro-goals to achieve macro-goals has served him well throughout his career, and chances are it will work well for you too.

EDMUND HILLARY
Mountaineer

Most people know that Edmund Hillary is the first man—along with Sherpa Tenzing Norgay—to reach the summit of Mount Everest. But what they don't know is that while that expedition made him world famous, it was only the beginning of his very busy, fulfilling, and successful life. In fact, it was what came after his first ascent of the world's highest peak that is truly his enduring legacy.

Born in New Zealand back in 1919, Hillary had a generally typical childhood. His home life was a fairly simple one, with his father working as a professional bee keeper while his mother tended to the children. For a time, it seemed Hillary was destined to follow in his father's footsteps and become a bee keeper himself, dabbling in the family business with his brother for a while. But he had dreams of exploring the world around him.

When he was a teenager, Hillary went on a class trip where he was introduced to climbing for the first time. He was immediately taken with the sport and would pursue it more actively while at university in Auckland. While there, he made his first major ascent, climbing to the summit of Mount Cook—New Zealand's highest peak at 12,218 feet.

For a time, Hillary's climbing ambitions were put on hold while he served in the Royal New Zealand Air Force during World War II, but after his stint in the military was over he returned to mountaineering, both at home and abroad.

In 1951, he took part in the British reconnaissance expedition to

Everest, which scouted a route to the summit along the Nepali side of the mountain for the very first time. That recon mission cleared the way for the Brits to return in 1953, which was when Hillary and Norgay finally completed the first successful ascent of the mountain.

While the duo did eventually make history on Everest, they weren't the first team chosen to go for the summit. In fact, two other members of the squad—Tom Bourdillon and Charles Evans—were given the first crack at the summit. When that pair failed to reach the top, Hillary and Norgay got the green light to make their attempt. Along the way, the two men managed to overcome a technical rock wall that was the final obstacle on their way to success. Later, that rock face would be named the "Hillary Step" and it has remained an important landmark on Everest ever since.

After overcoming that last remaining hurdle, Hillary and Norgay continued upwards, covering the final few hundred feet relatively quickly. The way to the summit was now clear and they would stand on the highest point on the planet at long last. For many years, neither man would say which of them got their first, but Norgay would eventually reveal that Hillary was a few steps in front of him on the final push.

There are no photos of Hillary on the summit that day, although there is a famous one of Norgay posing with his ice axe. At the time, the BBC claimed that was because the Nepali climber didn't know how to operate a camera. The reality was that Hillary declined to have his photos taken. He simply wanted to enjoy the view while it lasted and didn't need a picture to confirm that he had gone where no other man had gone before. He had achieved what he had set out to do, and taking a photo was the furthest thing from his mind. In our social media-obsessed modern age, more of us could learn a lesson from that.

Upon their return to Kathmandu, Hillary and Norgay found themselves to suddenly be two of the most famous men in the entire world. Their photo was plastered across the front page of every major newspaper and their accomplishment was celebrated across the globe. It was a startling change in lifestyle for a man who had never sought, nor felt comfortable, in the limelight. Later, when

Hillary returned home to New Zealand, a friend reportedly told him that the rest of his life would now be a comfortable one. He could sit back and enjoy a life of leisure, safe in the knowledge that his Everest climb would make him a wealthy man.

But Hillary wasn't interested in that kind of lifestyle. He had other things in mind and resting on his laurels wasn't a part of the plan. He couldn't just stay home and ignore all of the other goals he had set for himself. He wanted to keep climbing in the Himalayas, exploring distant lands, and helping the less fortunate of the world. There were far too many adventures yet to be had to just settle down prematurely.

Between 1956 and 1965, He would return to Nepal numerous times, climbing ten other peaks in the Himalayas. In 1958 he would also take part in an expedition that traveled to the South Pole using motorized vehicles for the very first time. Years later, he would also fly to the North Pole, becoming the first person to stand at both Poles, as well as on the summit of Everest. Once, he even led an expedition from sea-to-source along the Ganges River, using jet boats to travel for thousands of miles upstream to locate the starting point of that famous waterway deep in the Himalayan Mountains.

Hillary, however, was much more than just a mountaineer and an explorer. He was also a dedicated philanthropist who was deeply committed to helping the Sherpa people of Nepal. To that end, in 1960 he established the Himalayan Trust, a nonprofit organization that would go on to build dozens of schools, several hospitals, and even an airstrip in the Khumbu Valley, which sits at the foot of the mountain that made him famous. Those facilities have altered and enriched the lives of the people living there in truly important ways, improving their health and education dramatically.

Obviously there is a lot to admire about the first man to summit Everest. As a mountaineer he was strong, talented, and fearless. But those were qualities that Hillary took with him into the other aspects of his life too, as he waded into politics, world affairs, and environmental issues on occasion. He even served as New Zealand's High Commissioner to India for a time, spending more than four years living in Delhi.

Beyond that however, Hillary also displayed a great deal of compassion for the people who played a crucial role in making him a household name. Hillary's efforts helped countless Nepalis lead a better life through improved educational and health facilities. His contributions to that country were so great in fact, that in celebration of the fiftieth anniversary of the first ascent of the highest peak on the planet, the government of Nepal conferred honorary citizenship on the New Zealander. He was the first foreign national to earn such an honor.

Hillary passed away on January 11, 2008. When that news of his death was announced, flags across New Zealand were lowered to half-mast in honor of their fallen hero. But even in the final year of his life—at the age of eighty-seven—he was still doing adventurous things. At a time when most of us are definitely ready to start taking things easy, he was still traveling to the South Pole and making regular visits to Nepal.

History will no doubt always remember Hillary as the man who first climbed Everest. But his true contribution has always been, and will continue to be, the lasting impact he has had on the Nepali people. The Himalayan Trust accomplished remarkable things during his lifetime and continues to do so even today. In 2014, when an avalanche claimed the lives of sixteen Sherpas working on Everest, the Trust raised funds to help their families. A year later, when a devastating earthquake hit Nepal claiming thousands of lives, the organization was one of the first to help set up emergency shelters and provide essential supplies to the people living in the Khumbu Valley. The organization is also committed to completely rebuilding all of the schools and other facilities that were damaged during the natural disaster.

We should all strive to lead a life that is as rich and full as Hillary's was. Not only did he have grand adventures in the far corners of the globe, but he also served his country, and managed to create an organization that continues to have a positive impact on the lives of the people of Nepal long after he has passed. That is a worthy legacy indeed.

Chapter 4

LEARNING FROM FAILURE

"Success is not final; failure is not fatal: It is the courage to
continue that counts."

—Winston Churchill

Two of the most important qualities that a successful person can
have are perseverance and the ability to learn from their mistakes.
No one who has ever achieved any measure of success in their chosen field has done so without facing failure along the way. But it isn't
the fact that they stumbled in the pursuit of their goals that is important. Instead it is how they reacted to those setbacks that eventually
defines their story.

It's been said that Thomas Edison made more than a thousand
iterations of the lightbulb before he finally hit on a design that actually worked. Similarly, Abraham Lincoln lost eight elections and
oversaw two failed businesses before going on to become one of
the greatest presidents in American history. Even basketball great
Michael Jordan was cut from his high school team as a sophomore.

Of course, Edison, Lincoln, and Jordan all went on to achieve
great things in their chosen fields, and while their career paths were
very different from one another, they shared some key traits that
played a role in their success. Each of them worked extremely hard
and displayed a tenacity and resiliency that would allow them to overcome adversity. They also continued to learn new things throughout

their professional lives, including how to take the lessons of failure and use that knowledge to further fuel their ambitions.

The fear of failure is a major stumbling block that often prevents people from achieving their full potential. For some, the mere thought of not achieving their goals is so paralyzing that they may not even risk trying at all. Others will face a significant setback for the first time and end up abandoning their plans altogether. But in reality, those setbacks can be great learning opportunities that set us on the appropriate path to get to where we want to go. They can also go a long way towards teaching us about our own boundaries—both mental and physical—and how to push beyond them.

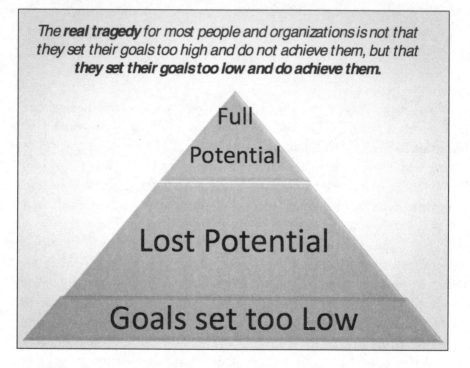

*The **real tragedy** for most people and organizations is not that they set their goals too high and do not achieve them, but that they set their goals too low and do achieve them.*

Full Potential

Lost Potential

Goals set too Low

In my case, after accomplishing any macro-goal that I set for myself, I tend to immediately begin looking for an even more challenging goal to go after next. My first macro-goal was to run a marathon, non-stop, without walking. This was a very daunting challenge since I was not yet a runner and didn't understand the commitment and dedication that went into proper training. I ran for less than three months before the Boston Marathon; that was all the running I had ever done in my entire life.

Once I had finished that race, I made a new macro-goal, to compete in a second marathon, within thirty days and to run it at least ten minutes faster, which I managed to accomplish as well. After every macro-goal was achieved the next macro-goal was even more challenging, pushing me to go faster or longer distances. Before long I grew into a very serious and competitive runner with times in the sub-2:50 range.

The list of macro-goals I have set for myself in life to date include:

Macro Goals Accomplished

- Navy SEAL
- SEAL Team SIX
- USG
- Hawaii IRONMAN
- Double IRONMAN
- Thirty Marathons/Ultras – Thirty-Six Months
- Work out everyday for over twenty years

- Compete in over a thousand endurance competitions
- Compete in the RAID Gauloises, "the World's Most Difficult Human Endurance Competition (eight to eleven days/three hundred and fifty to six hundred miles)
- Mountaineer
- Author

After competing in over one thousand endurance competitions, including marathons, ultramarathons, bike races, kayak races, and triathlons, I went in search of another challenge and found it in the form of a "Double Ironman." As the name implies, all of the distances in the event are double that of a standard Ironman, requiring competitors to swim 4.8 miles, ride 224 miles, and run 52.4 miles. For me, that seemed like the next logical step in my evolution as an ultra-distance endurance athlete. Since I was able to finish an

Ironman in less than twelve hours, I should be able to complete two Ironman races in less than a day, right? It seemed so logical to me at the time. I simply downgraded the Ironman to micro-goal status and made my new macro-goal to finish two Ironman races in a single day.

My Double Ironman experience didn't go quite as expected, although I would learn a lot about myself and my personal boundaries along the way. My training for the event went as planned, and while it was tough, I enjoyed the physical and mental challenges that came with longer distances. On race day, I took off as usual, and completed the first two stages at a fairly good pace. Transitioning from the swim to the bike went about as well as could be expected, and eventually I set out on the 52.4 mile run.

After the first twenty-six miles were complete, I thought to myself, only one more marathon to go, It wasn't many years before this that the marathon was the macro-goal, but this time out it was just one piece of a much bigger race. But thirty-two miles into the run things started to go bad. I felt beyond exhausted and completely sapped of energy. My legs and feet were crying out in pain and I was nearing my physical limits. My body began to break down from the demand that I had placed on it. I wasn't sure how much more I could take, but at the same time I was not about to quit either. I hadn't just hit the proverbial wall but had instead smashed right through it. In the parlance of endurance racers, I had "bonked," and bonked badly.

Bonking occurs when an athlete pushes him or herself so hard that it causes an almost total depletion of the glycogen stores in their body. When humans eat carbohydrates, they are typically converted into glycogen, which is then stored for use when we need a burst of energy. When that happens, glycogen is broken down and released into the bloodstream in the form of glucose, which serves as a source of fuel for our cells. During regular workouts and athletic competitions, our bodies tap into our glycogen reserves to provide the energy we need to push ourselves. But if we push too far, we may use up all of the glycogen we have in our bodies, leaving us feeling miserable and completely spent.

As my body began shutting down, I recognized the all-too-familiar signs and symptoms. First I started to see white spots or "stars," which is attributable to a lack of oxygen. Then I began to dry heave, hacking up green bile, while also experiencing double vision. It felt as though I was coughing up a rib. It was very painful. I stumbled onto the grass, fell down, and lost consciousness. When I came to, I felt disoriented and exhausted and couldn't understand why I was sleeping outside on the ground. As I watched other runners and cyclists passing me by, my brain struggled to comprehend what had happened. I was dazed and confused and couldn't make sense of the scene that was taking place around me.

It took some time to process the situation and determine exactly how I came to be lying face down on the grass. Eventually it struck me however; completely tapped out of energy, I had collapsed and had literally hit my physical limits. My body simply shut down. It was the only defense mechanism it had for giving me the break that I sorely needed.

Slowly but surely, I crawled back to my feet, even as every muscle in my body protested. I mustered up as much energy as I could and managed to resume running. My body wanted to stop but my mind kept telling me I hadn't finished what I had set out to do just yet. With that thought in my head I pressed on, dragging myself over the final twenty miles of the course until I reached the finish line.

Although I had reached my goal of finishing the Double Ironman, I couldn't help but feel a little disappointed. My performance during the race did not meet the expectations I had set for myself and I even collapsed and lost consciousness during the run. All things considered, it was hard to add that accomplishment to the "win" column.

But, I learned some very important lessons along the way. For instance, while my body might have given up, my mind hadn't. It remained strong, focused, and as determined as ever to finish the race. It was through sheer strength of will that I was able to get up off the ground and continue running the final stage of the event. This was a sharp reminder of the importance of having the right mindset and that remaining mentally tough was at least as important as being physically fit.

I had also learned that I could push my body to its absolute limits

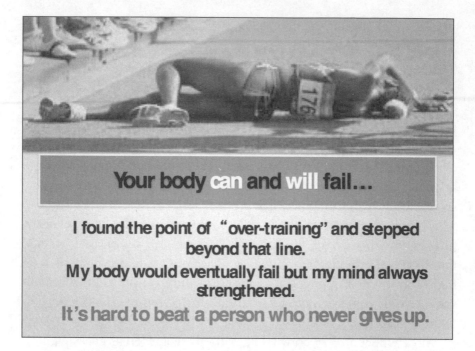

Your body can and will fail...

I found the point of "over-training" and stepped beyond that line.
My body would eventually fail but my mind always strengthened.
It's hard to beat a person who never gives up.

and if it needed a break, it would do me a favor and simply shut down for a while. If I was conscious, I could continue putting one foot in front of the other, no matter how painful it might be. But if that pain became too severe, I'd pass out and get some much-needed rest. It wasn't necessarily the ideal way to power my way through an endurance competition, but it was helpful to know that if need be, I could literally will myself to the finish the line.

Every one of us has a point where his or her body will fail, but we all are capable of making our minds stronger each and every day.

Bonking is extremely common amongst endurance athletes and most are forced to deal with it at some point during their athletic careers. My experience with hitting the wall in the Double Ironman taught me a good lesson. In all of the times prior to that race when I felt things were too hard or I was simply feeling sorry for myself, I discovered that I was wrong. I had learned that I could go farther than I had ever thought possible before, and I discovered where my boundaries were truly defined.

My accomplishments pale to many whom I have served with,

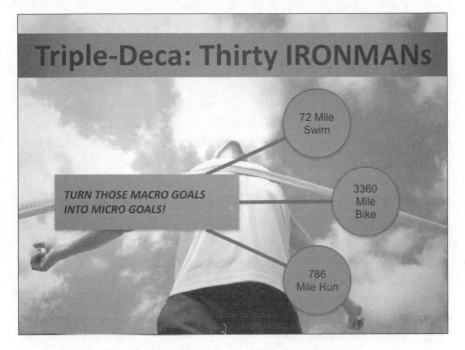

Triple-Deca: Thirty IRONMANs

TURN THOSE MACRO GOALS INTO MICRO GOALS!

72 Mile Swim

3360 Mile Bike

786 Mile Run

trained with, and competed against. Although I am proud to have finished a Double Ironman, there have been many triathletes who have done triple Ironman distance events, ten times Ironman distance events, and the longest to date at an incredible thirty times the distance. These are people just like you and me, men and women who want something bad enough that they can do what most others feel is impossible.

As I continued my endurance sports career, I would push myself even harder, particularly when I started competing in adventure races, which are often measured in days, rather than just a few hours. But knowing my own limits and understanding what my body could endure helped me to know when I could push myself harder and when I needed to back off.

Early in my career in sports, I felt that if I did not occasionally bonk, pass out, or hallucinate, I would never learn exactly where the limits of my mental and physical abilities could be found. Coming to understand those boundaries would become increasingly important as I took on even bigger challenges down the line, both in my athletic endeavors and as a Navy SEAL. Pain and suffering were all part of the process of reaching my goals, and it was that tough mindset that allowed me to continually overcome challenges. I learned to welcome the pain. As a young SEAL trainee going through BUDS, I would, with humility, look at the instructors and think, "Bring it on, I will take whatever you can dish out." If it is actually too much for me to take physically, my body will do me a favor and I will simply pass out. I learned to look at long races and challenging mountaineering expeditions in this very same way.

I believe we all owe it to ourselves to explore our own limits. If you want to reach your full potential, you'll need to push yourself to the edge of what you think is possible. Chances are, you will be surprised at what you can achieve once you begin to really test yourself. Just understand that when you aim high, you'll occasionally come up a little short. But what you learn from those experiences can prove incredibly valuable for both reaching your own goals and getting to know your strengths and limitations at the same time.

I believe there is an imaginary line that once you go over it, things will start breaking down. Relationships, marriages, performance at work or in school, and your bodily limits are all subject to negative consequences. I purposely went over this line on at least a monthly basis for decades and I pushed many teammates well over that line as well. My rational was that if you did not go over the line from time to time you could not be sure that you actually gave it your all. This is why SEAL instructors push potential candidates so hard. We don't care how strong, fit, fast, or gifted recruits are. We want to see who will take all that is dished out without quitting.

Above all else, it is important to learn from our mistakes, refocus on the mission, the dream, and the macro-goals we want to achieve, and keep moving forward. Failure doesn't mean that your goal is out of reach; it only means that it may require a different path to get there. Try not to let yourself dwell on the things that went wrong for too long, but instead focus on the things that went right. The lessons we learn from failure come from knowing what worked and what didn't. Then you can incorporate the positive things when moving forward.

Failure isn't the opposite of success but is actually a part of it. If you set a major goal for yourself, it probably shouldn't be easy to achieve, and more than likely you're going to stumble along the way. But perseverance, focus, and an ability to learn from previous mistakes can unlock the road to achieving even the loftiest of macro-goals.

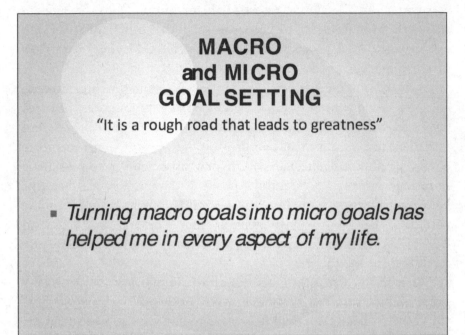

MACRO
and MICRO
GOAL SETTING

"It is a rough road that leads to greatness"

- *Turning macro goals into micro goals has helped me in every aspect of my life.*

This is something that high-altitude mountaineers know better than just about anyone else. For them, failure is often a part of the process, with many climbers returning to the same peak multiple times before actually cracking the code that allows them to reach the summit. Success in the mountains requires equal parts skill, experience, and preparation, with a healthy dose of luck thrown in for good measure. But even when climbers do everything right, including selecting a safe route, bringing all of the necessary gear, and training properly ahead of time, they can have variables beyond their control that prevent them from reaching the top. Poor weather conditions often put a halt to an expedition, and unexpected illness or injury can frequently send climbers home without achieving their intended objectives. But each step forward is a positive one that could eventually hold the key to future success.

Nowhere is that more evident than on Mount Everest. In 1952, the race was on to be the first person to reach the summit of the world's highest peak. For more than thirty years British mountaineers had enjoyed exclusive access to the mountain from the Tibetan side of the Himalayas, but when China claimed sovereignty over that country in 1950, it closed its borders to outsiders, leaving the English scrambling to find other options.

A year later, Nepal issued its first ever permit to climb Everest, allowing reconnaissance missions to scout the mountain's southern flanks for the very first time. A potentially safe route to the summit was identified by a British team in the fall of 1951, with members of the expedition planning to return the following spring to make a serious attempt at reaching the summit. Unfortunately for them the Nepali government had already awarded the one and only climbing permit for that year to a Swiss team instead. The Brits would have to wait their turn for once and watch as another team of alpinists took a crack at the mountain.

As with most expeditions through the Himalayas, the Swiss decided to hire local Sherpa guides and porters to serve as support staff both in base camp and higher up the mountain. Even then the Sherpa peoples had a reputation for being hard working and dependable, particularly at high altitude. It didn't take long for several of the locals to prove indispensable to their Swiss teammates. A few Sherpas had even been a part of past British Everest expeditions, including a guide named Tenzing Norgay, who had been on Everest in 1935, 1936, and again in 1947. As a result, he had spent more time at high altitude than virtually anyone else on the planet.

Much to the surprise of the Swiss climbers, their efforts on Everest went better than expected. Using intel that had been gathered by the British a year earlier, they were able to clear the dangerous Khumbu Icefall, scale the Western Cwm, and make their way up the South Col for the first time. The route that they had pioneered would eventually become the same one that is used by the majority of climbers today, but in 1952 it was almost completely unexplored.

After spending several weeks acclimatizing and preparing for the ascent, three Europeans, along with their trusted and valuable guide, Tenzing Norgay, set off for the top of the mountain. They made slow, but steady progress, and eventually established high camp at 27,600 feet. It was at that point that two of the Swiss climbers elected to turn back. Exhausted and pushed to their physical limits, they knew it was unwise to go any higher. So, they bid their companions good luck and turned down the mountain.

The remaining Swiss climber was a man named Raymond Lambert and over the course of the expedition, he and Norgay had become close friends. The duo spent a long, cold, and difficult night at their campsite with no sleeping bags, no stoves, and only a simple tent to protect them from the elements. Huddling together for warmth, they passed the lonely hours by melting ice and snow over a candle to produce a bit of drinking water to keep them hydrated, something which is always a challenge at high altitude.

The following morning Lambert and Norgay set off once again, heading up into the unknown. They were embarking on what was truly the first legitimate attempt to reach the summit of Everest via the South Face in Nepal, and the route above them remained entirely uncharted. They weren't quite sure what they would find, but they climbed on nevertheless.

Although the conditions were favorable and both men felt fine that day, they ultimately failed to reach the summit due to faulty equipment. The oxygen masks that they had depended upon quit working and for several hours they were essentially climbing without the use of bottled oxygen, which was vital to their efforts. At times they even resorted to crawling on all fours to make progress, as the heavy weight of useless equipment sapped their strength. Eventually they too were forced to admit defeat and turn back, joining their companions in base camp.

Although the Swiss expedition hadn't achieved its goal of reaching the summit, their time on the mountain wasn't a complete loss. They learned that the oxygen tanks that they carried with them had a major design flaw that prevented them from working properly while the climbers were moving. That flaw would be fixed in future iterations, allowing mountaineers to safely go higher than they had ever gone before. The two men has also managed to reach a height of 28,199 feet, and still got back down safely. At the time, that was a new altitude record for any human being, coming within just 830 feet of the highest point on the planet.

The team returned home with a treasure trove of knowledge not only about the route that led to the summit, but the gear that would be necessary to complete the ascent too. They gained important insights about how the human body reacts to high altitude and in the process pushed themselves to their very limits—and in some cases beyond. The team's experience would pave the way for many expeditions that followed, creating a template for high-altitude climbing in the Himalayas that remains largely the same to this day. In other words, their failure became the building blocks to success for those that followed.

Tenzing Norgay, the Sherpa guide who played such an instrumental role for the Swiss team, would return to Everest a year later as part of yet another British expedition. Eventually he would be paired up with a modest and unassuming bee keeper from New Zealand by the name of Edmund Hillary and the duo would be assigned "second team" status, waiting their turn for a crack at the mountain while others made the attempt first. When the lead team was unable to complete the ascent, Hillary and his Sherpa teammate were given the green light to have a go at the summit, eventually writing their place in the history books.

On May 29, 1953 Hillary and Norgay became the first men to ever step foot on the top of Mount Everest. For decades, neither of them would confirm who was the first to reach the summit, as they were a team from start to finish. Both men were strong climbers, but it was Norgay's knowledge of the mountain and experience at high altitude that provided them with the edge that they needed to succeed.

As part of the failed expedition from a year earlier, Norgay was able to return to the mountain with all of the intel that the Brits would need to finally reach the top. He could provide firsthand information about the route and he knew how to overcome most of the obstacles in their path. The long night that he and Lambert spent in their tent at 27,600 feet was also an important part of his experience, reminding him that he and Hilary could enhance their chances of success by carrying more gear with them at altitude. Perhaps most importantly of all, the British team came armed with improved oxygen masks, making subtle improvements to the system that had failed only a year earlier.

Following their success on Everest, Hillary and Norgay became instant celebrities who were recognizable in nearly every corner of the globe. Although it had taken thirty years and numerous attempts, the highest mountain on the planet had been conquered at last, and it made headlines around the world. Although all previous attempts had ended in failure, each of them provided insight and information that would prove invaluable to the climbers that followed. The Sherpa and the beekeeper benefited from that knowledge and were the first to actually put all of the pieces together, allowing them to solve the puzzle that was Everest.

Ed Viestur is another high altitude mountaineer who knows how difficult it can be to climb in the Himalayas. I had the chance to spend some time with Ed during my own expedition to Everest in 2016 and found him to be a friendly, modest man who is very low-key about his own accomplishments in the mountains. For being one of the most accomplished alpinists in history you wouldn't know it by his demeanor.

To date, Ed is the only American to summit all fourteen of the world's 8,000-meter peaks, doing so without the use of bottled oxygen. Those mountains include not only the formidable Everest and K2, but a peak named Annapurna as well. That particular mountain is amongst the most dangerous in the entire world and would become Viesturs's nemesis, pushing him to his very limits on more than one occasion.

Born in Indiana and raised in Illinois, Viesturs began his life as a lowlander. In high school he discovered a book entitled *Annapurna*, written by the famous French mountaineer Maurice Herzog. In that account, Herzog tells the story of the first ascent of the titular mountain, which was first conquered in 1950. The book itself is widely considered to be one of the most influential mountaineering stories ever written, inspiring a generation of alpinists that followed. Viesturs would become one of those climbers.

While *Annapurna* had put wild tales of expeditions to the Himalayas in his head as a teenager, Viesturs wouldn't seriously start climbing until he moved to Seattle to attend college in 1977. While at the University of Washington studying to become a veterinarian, he began making excursions up nearby mountains, summiting Mount St. Helens a couple of years before the volcano's famous eruption in 1980. He would also spend a considerable amount of time on Mount Rainier as well, gaining the skills and experience he needed to take on major climbs elsewhere in the world. Eventually he would become a guide on that mountain, reaching its summit more than two hundred times across the course of his career.

In 1989, Viesturs made his first expedition to the Himalayas, successfully knocking off Kangchenjunga, the third highest mountain in the world. Over the next couple of years, he'd summit Everest and K2 as well, adding the tallest and second tallest peaks on the planet to his resume. It was about that time that he seriously started considering climbing the remaining 8,000-meter mountains, but he knew if he undertook that challenge, he'd want to do it without using supplemental oxygen, something that only a handful of other climbers had ever accomplished.

When high altitude mountaineers venture up above 26,000 feet, they enter what is commonly called "the death zone." At that height, the air is so thin that there isn't enough oxygen for them to survive for extended periods of time, which causes the body to begin to shut down. That's why the vast majority of climbers on Everest and other major peaks wear oxygen tanks and masks when they launch their summits bids. Without those tanks, a climber's lungs can only manage to pull in about 30 percent of the oxygen that they can at sea level.

But some of the more physically gifted and talented climbers will forego the use of bottled oxygen to add yet another level of challenge to their climb. Those men and women are able to continue to perform at a high level even at extreme altitudes, although they are always aware that they are in a race against time. Eventually their bodies will need to get back to the more oxygen-rich atmosphere found below 8,000-meters or they'll simply perish on the mountain.

That was a risk that Viesturs was willing to take to achieve his goal. For him, climbing without oxygen was the purest approach to the sport, pitting man against mountain on the fairest terms possible. Ed had always approached high altitude mountaineering with the attitude that if he couldn't get to the top without using bottled oxygen, he probably didn't deserve to be there anyway—a somewhat radical mindset back in the early 1990s.

Still, Viesturs found plenty of success doing it his way. He systematically began checking off the 8,000-meter peaks one after another, all without ever needing to use supplemental oxygen. He had already proven himself to be an incredibly gifted and strong climber, but his determination, keen mind, and thorough planning now put him in a class reserved for only the greatest of alpinists. It seemed that his quest to climb the fourteen tallest mountains on the planet was assured of success. That is, until he got to Annapurna.

In 2000, Viesturs made his first expedition to the mountain that had inspired him to become a climber in the first place. He approached Annapurna like any other climb, setting up a series of camps along its flank, acclimatizing to the altitude, and preparing to make his ascent to the summit. That was the process that had worked many times in the past, including multiple times on Everest.

But Annapurna isn't like other 8,000-meter peaks. Standing 26,545 feet in height, it is the tenth highest mountain on the planet. Its main summit is flanked by more than two dozen other massive peaks, a number of which stand above 23,000 feet themselves. Its steep walls are imposing to look upon, and the weather is notoriously fickle, with high winds and extremely cold temperatures, even in base camp. Persistent storms often dump heavy snow across the region, which can lead to instability along the summit route, causing dangerous avalanches that have been known to sweep climbers over the edge. In fact, so many mountaineers have perished on Annapurna that it holds the dubious distinction of having the highest fatality rate of any 8,000-meter peak, making it far more dangerous than Everest.

Viesturs and his team witnessed these dangerous conditions first hand. While making their summit bid on the North Side of the mountain, they came to realize that all of the routes to the top were choked with heavy snow, most of which was highly unstable. If they pressed on, there was a good chance they could trigger an avalanche, which would almost certainly send them plummeting thousands of feet down a sheer cliff face. Known for his conservative climbing style, Viesturs elected to pull the plug on the expedition and go home without reaching the summit. It was the wise and safe decision, even if it meant admitting defeat.

Two years later, he returned to Annapurna to attempt a different route, this time trying his luck on the South Side of the mountain instead. But upon approaching 24,000 feet, he once again encountered conditions that were simply too dangerous and difficult to continue upwards. The avalanche risk was even higher than on his previous visit to the mountain and several close calls were a sharp reminder of just how dangerous Annapurna truly was. Discretion was once again the better part of valor, and Viesturs left Annapurna without reaching the top for a second time.

By 2005, Ed had achieved his goal of summiting all of the 8,000-meter peaks without the use of bottled oxygen, save one. The summit of Annapurna remained elusive, and he was beginning to wonder if he'd ever be able to add the mountain to his list of accomplishments. At the time, he wasn't even sure if he wanted to go back and face the same risks and challenges once again. He had flirted with disaster twice in the past and was lucky enough to safely return home relatively unscathed. Would he be pushing his luck if he returned for a third time?

But his goal wasn't to summit thirteen of the fourteen tallest mountains in the world—it was to get them all. That meant that if he wanted to add his name to the elite list of climbers who had accomplished that same feat, he was going to have to go back to Annapurna one more time. He had failed on his two previous attempts but came away with a better understanding of what he had to do in order to be successful. Despite that however, the mountain would not go down without a fight.

After spending several weeks acclimatizing to the altitude, shuttling gear to high camp, and preparing for the ascent, Viesturs set off for the top. But as he climbed up to 22,500 feet, the weather took a turn for the worse, with high winds buffeting the upper sections of the mountain, completely sealing off the summit.

Once again, it appeared as if Annapurna's constantly shifting weather would prevent the American climber from achieving his goal. For three long days, Viesturs and his teammates huddled together in their tents waiting for the winds to subside. At times, it seemed like they would have no choice but to turn back, as the gusts rattled their tiny shelters for hours on end. All they could do was wait to see if things improved enough for them to take a crack at the summit.

Eventually the winds did die down and the team set off for the top. It would take eleven hours to cover 4,000 vertical feet, but on May 12, 2005 Ed Viesturs found himself on the summit of his final 8,000-meter peak at long last. The mountain that had initially inspired him to begin his climbing career had served as his nemesis too, luring him back multiple times despite the incredible dangers. That only made Viesturs's eventual success all the sweeter, reminding him that most things that are worth achieving in life rarely come easy.

In finally conquering Annapurna, Viesturs also accomplished his macro-goal of climbing the fourteen highest peaks on the planet, becoming the first American to achieve that feat. It took him sixteen long years to complete that task, which serves as a reminder that there are few overnight success stories. Achieving a big goal often takes time, dedication, planning, and an ability to bounce back from adversity. It took him three attempts to finally unlock the secret to success on Annapurna, but ultimately he was able to do just that, leaving his own mark on mountaineering history in the process.

Ed's story certainly left its mark on me as well, serving as inspiration for my own climbing ambitions. When he and I were together on Everest I had the chance to get to know him some and was incredibly impressed by his quiet confidence and upbeat attitude. He had so much energy and enthusiasm, and was so happy to be back on the mountain. It was a real honor for me to spend some time with that great man.

Mountaineers require a different kind of strength, endurance, and mental toughness than most other athletes, which is why I naturally found myself gravitating towards the sport in the beginning of my athletic career. After competing in countless marathons, ultramarathons, triathlons, and adventure races, alpine climbing represented the next big challenge, and I soon found my macro-goals focused on summiting difficult peaks all over the world, including Everest.

My mountaineering career would end up taking me to some far-flung corners of the globe including the Himalayas, the Andes, the Rockies, and beyond. In South America, I reached the summit on iconic volcanos like Cotopaxi and Cayambe, and in Africa I trekked up Kilimanjaro, the tallest mountain on that continent. Back home in the States I topped out on Mount Whitney in California, Longs Peak in Colorado, and the Grand Teton in Wyoming. Along the way,

Feeling so strong and determined to summit Mount Everest
2014 and 2015 Everest's Most Deadly Years

I summited numerous 14,000-foot peaks across the American West as well as dozens more in places like Ethiopia, Patagonia, South Korea, and South Africa.

Perhaps my crowning achievement in the mountains came with a successful summit of Denali (Mount McKinley) in Alaska. As the tallest peak in North America, Denali draws hundreds of climbers on an annual basis, but due to its extremely unpredictable weather, it is a difficult climb even during the height of the Alaskan summer. Because it is such a technical challenge, and sits at such a high longitudinal geographic location, the 20,310-foot mountain is commonly used as a tune-up for Everest. Many mountaineers with bigger aspirations come to Denali to test their strength and skill there before proceeding on to the Himalayas.

For more than twenty-five years Everest had been my ultimate macro-goal. To me, scaling the tallest mountain on Earth was a challenge unlike any other, requiring climbers to not only be physically fit but mentally tough as well. It is an undertaking that requires not just stamina and skill, but patience, resiliency, and determination.

In the spring of 2016 I traveled to Nepal to finally attempt this massive undertaking. It was a trying time for Everest, as just two years earlier an avalanche had killed sixteen Nepalese guides, shocking the mountaineering community and bringing an abrupt end to the climbing season. At the time, that was the single biggest disaster in the long history of the mountain. Just one year later things would get much worse.

On April 25, 2015 a massive earthquake rocked Nepal, claiming the lives of more than 9,000 people, including twenty-two climbers who were in base camp on the South Side of Everest at the time. Once again, the spring climbing season was cancelled, leaving a great deal of uncertainty as to the future of commercial expeditions to the mountain. Was it simply too difficult and dangerous to climb Everest anymore? Were these back-to-back disasters a harbinger of things to come?

All climbers know the inherent risks of climbing Everest: there are dangerous crevasses, shifting ice and rock, avalanches, hypothermia, frostbite, altitude sickness, high altitude cerebral, and pulmonary edema—the list goes on. I was willing to accept those risks however, knowing full well what I was getting myself into.

Thankfully, the 2016 season went off without a hitch and was actually one of the most successful years in Everest history. Hundreds of people reached the summit, ushering in a new sense of optimism not only for the mountain, but for the future of Nepal as well. Unfortunately however, I wasn't among those who found success on Everest that year. Instead, I found myself fighting for my life.

For any climber attempting Everest from the South Side, the expedition first begins with a ten-day hike just to reach base camp. That trek helps to jumpstart the acclimatization process, allowing your body to slowly become accustomed to the thinner air that is experienced at altitude. Throughout the trek I felt strong, well-conditioned, and completely prepared for the challenges ahead.

It isn't until you reach base camp at 17,600 feet that the work truly begins. In order to continue to acclimatize to the altitude, climbers will go up the mountains, spending a night or two at a series of increasingly higher camps, before returning to base camp to recover. The entire process takes several weeks to complete, but once it is done, your body is much better prepared to go to for the summit.

Directly above base camp on the Nepali side of the mountain is one of the most notoriously dangerous sections of the climb. The Khumbu Icefall is a confusing maze of rock and ice that is created by the calving of a nearby glacier. The blue-ice towers that make up the icefall have been known to crumble, crack, and collapse with very little warning, making it a precarious area to navigate. To cross through this section of the climb, a series of ladders are placed over the crevasses that open up between the pillars of ice. The climbers then use those ladders as makeshift bridges that allow them to walk over the gaping chasms below on their way up to camp 1.

It was during one of my trips through the Khumbu Icefall that I ran into trouble. I began choking and coughing as I slowly but surely made my way upwards, crossing the sixteen-foot aluminum ladders that had been carefully put into place over the open crevasses. At the time, I knew that I wasn't feeling particularly well, but I thought I

16 foot aluminum ladders (1- 6)

may have simply contracted a bad case of the "Khumbu cough," a bronchial condition that is brought on by overexertion and exposure of the lung to cold air at higher altitudes. The Khumbu cough is annoying and frustrating, but it isn't particularly dangerous, and I thought that it would pass with time.

By the time I had cleared the icefall and had began making my way up to Camp 1, where we planned to spend the night, things started to get worse. My incessant coughing made it even more difficult to breathe in the thin air, and it was becoming increasingly more exhausting trying to put one foot in front of the other. It was clear that I was battling something other than just a simple cough, but I didn't know just how serious my condition actually was. That is, until I continued to climb higher and the world around me went black.

I lost my color vision, my memory, and my sense of direction. I told my climbing team to go ahead without me, that I would be right behind them. I just needed a small break to catch my breath. I ended up passing out. When I woke up I saw my team way off in the distance. I could barely make out their figures or count how many of them were there.

A very experienced guide from New Zealand named Mike Roberts, who has summited Everest on seven separate occasions, realized I had fallen way behind the rest of the team and came to my rescue. He immediately recognized that I was suffering and may not get off the mountain alive. He gave me his oxygen and we made it back to base camp.

With every breath I would exhale my mask would fill with fluids. The sound of my breath was loud and gurgling, as I was literally drowning in my own fluids. Days before one of our lead Sherpas and our doctor were medevac'd off the mountain with the same condition, although not as severe.

Mike went to other tents at base camp looking for someone who could lend a hand. He located a female doctor who was injured during the avalanche in 2015. Her leg was ripped open when a rock had hit her. She sutured her own leg and went on to treat the wounded and care for the dead. I was extremely honored to be treated by this woman even though she did tell me, in a very professional manner, that I needed to get off of the mountain or I would not survive.

The weather got bad that evening and we could not get a helicopter to come in for my rescue. I survived the night while managing to keep all of my teammates up with my choking and coughing. The next morning, I made the painful trek—using bottled oxygen—to the landing zone and was picked up and flown to a hospital in Katmandu.

I have only vague memories of that rescue operation and my flight off Everest. When I regained full consciousness, I was in a hospital being treated for a severe case of acute mountain sickness (AMS), which includes symptoms like headaches, nausea, and extreme fatigue.

But AMS was the least of my worries. The doctor told me that I was also suffering from both high altitude cerebral edema (HACE) and pulmonary edema (HAPE), which meant fluid was collecting in my lungs and developing on my brain. Left untreated, HACE and HAPE are extremely dangerous, often resulting in death. In fact, the doctor said that if I had stayed on the mountain one more day, or had climbed any higher, I would have died there on the slopes of Everest.

> # ONE OF THE GREATEST TRAGEDIES OF LIFE IS NOT DEATH, BUT WHAT WE LET DIE INSIDE OF US WHILE WE LIVE.

It was a sobering end to my dream of scaling the tallest mountain on the planet, and yet I learned some valuable lessons from that experience. It was one of the few times in my life that I ever came face-to-face with my own physical limits; it very nearly killed me. That alone was enough to make me pause and reassess my goals and the risks involved when pursuing them.

Even as fit and strong as I was, it wasn't enough to overcome the inherent risks and challenges that came along with climbing at high altitude. I had trained as well as I could, I was mentally and physically prepared for the challenge, and I had all of the gear and equipment necessary to reach the summit, and yet it still wasn't enough. I took solace in knowing that while my body may have quit, my mind had remained as strong and focused as ever. Coming up short due to physical circumstances beyond my control was something I could live with but giving up mentally was completely unacceptable.

When looking back on my own Everest aspirations, I am reminded once again of Ed Viesturs, who has climbed that same mountain seven times throughout his career. He has famously said that when it came to his own climbing expeditions he operated under one important rule: "Reaching the summit is optional. Getting down is mandatory." The summit of the mountain was indeed my macrogoal, but coming home to friends and family is perhaps the most important goal of all.

On Everest, I learned just how far I could actually go and while that may not have been all the way to the summit, my near-death experience there has helped me to redefine my expectations for other challenges to come.

I feel so very fortunate that I had this experience. I certainly did not want to only dream of climbing Everest, I truly wanted to give it a try. Although my body did not cooperate, I came home, made a full recovery, and I survived. Seven climbers died who were with us in base camp. Many of them suffered the same symptoms I had. They were higher up on the mountain and were not able to get down safely. It was heart-breaking to learn how they were suffering and to know they were not coming home. Many of their bodies remain on the mountain with the 200-plus others who have perished there over the years.

WINSTON CHURCHILL
Politician

Most people know Winston Churchill as the masterful British prime minister who defied Nazi Germany during World War II and helped lead the Allies to victory in Europe. History tends to regard him as one of the preeminent statesmen of the twentieth century, leading his country through one of its most precarious moments and helping to rebuild after the war. But Churchill's career didn't get off to such an impressive start. In fact, his first foray into leadership went so poorly that he was forced to resign from office and retreat from public life for a time.

Born in England on November 30, 1874, Churchill would begin his service to his country at the age of twenty when he joined the British Army. This career choice would take him all over the world, participating in military actions in India, Sudan, South Africa, and Spain. He even visited Cuba during its war of independence and spent some time in the US along the way too.

Although born to an aristocratic family and educated in fine schools, Churchill came to believe that he was lacking in knowledge compared to other persons with whom he found himself interacting. While stationed in India he took it upon himself to rectify this situation by reading the works of Plato, Aristotle, Charles Darwin, Adam Smith, and other great thinkers. He studied ancient history, philosophy, and the natural sciences, all in an effort to expand his knowledge with the hopes that it would pay off for him in the long run. Even as a young man, Churchill had political ambitions and he didn't want deficiencies in his education to come back to haunt him.

In 1900, at the age of twenty five, Churchill ran for parliament, winning a seat in a very close election. This launched what would become a long career in government which include stints as the president of the Board of Trade, the home secretary, and the first lord of the Admiralty. That was the position he held at the outbreak of World War I and would ultimately lead to his resignation following a slew of controversial decisions and very public defeats at the hands of the enemy.

The worst of those defeats came at Gallipoli, a strategic peninsula that belonged to the Ottoman Empire, in what is now modern day Turkey. Churchill had proposed a naval assault of Gallipoli followed by an amphibious landing to capture this section of land. But the campaign went poorly from the beginning, with Allied forces taking heavy casualties and the Brits losing several key battleships. It was a complete disaster that would follow Churchill for years and force him to resign his position in disgrace.

Following such a public humiliation, most people would have looked to disappear from the radar and lay low for a bit. But Churchill isn't most people and he wasn't content to just sit on the sidelines. Instead, he reenlisted in the British Army and was sent to the Eastern Front. There he served with distinction, first leading a small unit on highly successful missions, which soon led to promotions that allowed him to have an even bigger impact on the battlefield. At the time, there was no more dangerous place on the planet, nor any better place for Churchill to rebuild his reputation.

In 1917, as the war was winding down, Churchill returned to parliament and was later appointed to the position of Secretary of State for War and Secretary of State for Air. Later, he would also play an instrumental role in rebuilding the UK's post-war economy, helping to lead the reconstruction process.

In 1929, Churchill's Conservative Party lost the elections and the fifty-five-year old found himself out of the limelight. Worse yet, when he chose to side with King Edward VIII during the abdication crisis of 1936, he found himself on the wrong side of public opinion. For a time, it looked like the roller coaster political career was over at long last as friends, supporters, and party officials distanced themselves from the politician.

Later, Churchill was one of a few men in the British government who recognized the growing threat that a rearmed Germany was posing in Europe. He spoke out vigorously against Hitler and his militaristic regime even before that became popular sentiment. This led to his return to his position as first lord of the Admiralty in 1939, more than twenty years after he first held that post during the First World War.

Less than a year later he would take over the office of Prime Minister following the resignation of Neville Chamberlain, who proved ineffective in dealing with the Germans or the escalating war effort. From there, Churchill would lead the UK throughout the rest of the Second World War, guiding the country through its darkest hour. As a wartime leader, Churchill proved to be shrewd, pragmatic, and to have a keen strategic mind. He welcomed his country's growing relationship with the United States and tolerated a much-needed alliance with the Soviet Union. And when the war was over, he helped organize the rebuilding process.

In the summer of 1945 British voters determined that the man who led them during the war was not the same man they wanted to lead them in peace. The Conservative Party lost the elections once again, and it looked like Churchill's career was finally at an end. But, he would return to 10 Downing Street to serve as Prime Minister once again from 1951-55 before finally riding off into the sunset at long last.

It is tough to think about any modern leader who faced more challenges throughout his career than Winston Churchill. He played instrumental roles in two world wars, helped rebuild Europe not once, but twice, and saw his own political fortunes rise and fall and rise again numerous times. Through it all, he remained steadfastly dedicated to serving the British people, acting as an unwavering force during the country's most trying times.

Churchill is the perfect example of someone who was able to find ways to overcome failure and continue moving forward. More than once in his long political career it looked as if he was finished. Yet every time he was counted out, he found a way to regain power and advance further up the ranks. He knew that adversity is a part of life, but it is how you adapt and learn from it that ultimately decides your fate. When he resigned following the disastrous Gallipoli campaign, he went off to the Eastern Front to rebuild his status. And when he made political missteps, he worked tirelessly to overcome the damage to his reputation and regain lost prestige and position.

Throughout his career, Churchill also proved that he could learn from his mistakes. His mismanagement of the military during WWI was not repeated during WWII. In fact, the lessons he learned proved invaluable when he became Prime Minister. And while other members of his party were looking to appease Hitler and the Nazi regime, Churchill spoke out against them, recognizing that an old threat had reappeared in a new guise.

A good politician is smart, wise, adaptable, and holds firm in his beliefs and commitments. Winston Churchill was all of that and so much more. He was the elder statesmen of the twentieth century, and when he passed away in 1965 he was given a state funeral as befitting his status. That funeral was attended by representatives of 112 countries and at the time it was the largest in history. Churchill himself became the first British commoner to lie in state in more than sixty-five years and the Royal Artillery provided him with a nineteen-gun salute. The streets of London were lined with mourners who came out to pay tribute to this legendary man for the final time.

Churchill's legacy is still felt in many ways in his home country and he still serves as an inspiration to millions around the world. We could all learn something about how to carry on after failure and continue looking for ways to overcome adversity on our way to reaching our objectives. He did that better than just about anyone, and accomplished enough in his lifetime to fill dozens of history books.

In 1941, with the war effort taking its toll on the British people, Churchill gave what would become his most famous speech. In it, he encouraged his countrymen to "never give up," spurring a great sense of pride and nationalism in those who listened. That same phrase could have easily been a motto for his entire life, as he was never one to give up, even when faced with what seemed like insurmountable adversity. That is one of many things that made him a special person, who never once gave up on himself, even during his own darkest hours.

Chapter 5

LEARNING FROM SUCCESS

"Success does not consist in never making mistakes but in never making the same one a second time."

–George Bernard Shaw

As we saw in the previous chapter, the ability to learn from failure can play a significant role in achieving our goals. After all, the road to success is rarely straight, and we should expect more than a few setbacks along the way. The things we take away from those failures usually end up making us stronger, smarter, and more resilient in the end. Plus, finding ways to overcome those obstacles is often the catalyst we need to put us on the path to achieving our goals.

Unfortunately, a successful venture doesn't always result in the same level of introspection and self-assessment that failure does. Often times, we're so happy and proud of achieving our goals that we forget to take a moment to reflect on what we've accomplished and just how exactly we got there in the first place. This can sometimes lead to the false assumption that we know everything that we need to reach our goals, and if we just repeat the same process over and over again we will continue to find success.

Of course, we all know that isn't necessarily true, but if we start to buy into that thought process, it can lead to complacency and stagnation—two things that can kill all of your momentum. By evaluating the things that went right, and considering the choices you made along the way, you may find that even though you were successful, there might have been a smarter, more efficient way to get to the finish line. That could prove invaluable when pursuing future goals, even if they are completely unrelated to one another.

One of the key differences that comes from learning from success rather than learning from failure has to do with what it is we're evaluating exactly. When we examine our failures, we tend to look at all of the things that went wrong, and then search for a silver lining to take away something positive from the experience. In this way, we identify mistakes, but also look for things we did right, even though our choices still ultimately resulted in failure.

But when it comes time to learn from our successes, we are mainly evaluating the things that went right while still searching for ways to improve upon the process. In this way, the learning process is a much more positive experience, often providing affirmation that we are on the right track, even as we refine our approach to reaching our goals. This often leads to increased confidence that we can achieve even bigger things down the line.

Confidence can be a very powerful tool when it comes to building mental toughness and achieving our goals. Simply believing that you can achieve the things you set out to accomplish can go a very long way towards overcoming the obstacles that are placed in front of us. Someone who lacks confidence may be tentative in their decision making or will simply give up when faced with adversity. On the other hand, those who have found some measure of success tend to have more confidence in themselves, which leads to decisive decision making, an increased conviction that they can overcome challenges, and a stricter adherence to a plan of action that they've developed. Those are all important ingredients in a classic recipe for success.

For the person who sets a goal of running a marathon, and then finally achieves that feat, examining their success is crucial to improving their performance in future competitions. For instance, when taking a look at all of the steps that they took to complete the marathon, they might discover that their training regimen and nutritional requirements were well balanced and effective but could still be tweaked to help improve their final results. Perhaps if the runner had reduced their mileage a bit in the final weeks, their legs would have been better rested going into the race. Or they may find that the diet they consumed leading up to the marathon could have benefited from increased proteins and carbohydrates, providing more fuel on race day.

In this example, the runner has already achieved what they set out to do—run a marathon—but in examining their success, they've also uncovered ways to improve their training and preparation for the next race. They've learned from the experience, discovered ways to become a more efficient runner, and are determined to adjust the formula moving forward in an effort to improve their overall performance. They've also more than likely gained a nice boost to their confidence simply by having a race under their belt, which not only eliminates some of the unknowns that come along with setting such a goal, but also answers the question of whether or not they could actually run the full distance.

Essentially, that's how it worked for me. After finishing my first marathon, it felt incredible to have achieved my goal of running twenty-six-plus miles without stopping, which had seemed nearly impossible just a few short months earlier. But, when I reflected on my performance in the race, I realized there was still plenty of room for improvement.

This led to a new macro-goal of improving my marathon times, allowing me to shave off more than forty minutes over the course of the following year. The confidence I gained from that experience helped me to continue to push myself as an endurance athlete, and soon left me looking for new challenges. I found them in the form of triathlon, a sport that combines three of my favorite activities: swimming, cycling, and running. It seemed like a sport that was tailor made for me, and it wasn't long before I was competing at a high level in "tri" events too. It was right about then that I started to hear rumblings about Ironmans, and before I knew it a completely new macro-goal had been created.

The original Ironman Triathlon sprung from a debate that had raged for years between runners and swimmers in Hawaii. Both groups routinely argued over which sport had the superior athletes, with the two sides pointing out the rigorous demands of their preferred activity. But at an awards ceremony honoring some of the local jocks, Navy commander John Collins proposed that perhaps cyclists were actually the best conditioned athletes of all, pointing out that legendary pro rider Eddy Merckx had recorded the highest VO2 max ever measured. (A VO2 max score is an indication of how much oxygen an athlete can effectively use while competing in a sport and is commonly seen as a sign of aerobic efficiency.)

Collins, who was already a triathlete himself, suggested that they settle the debate once and for all by combining three established local ultra-distance endurance events into a single massive challenge. Those events included the 2.4-mile Rough Water swim, the Around-Oahu bike race, which covered 115 miles, and the 26.2-mile Honolulu Marathon. The start and ending point for the bike race would eventually be adjusted slightly to accommodate the course, resulting in a 112 mile bike ride instead, which is how the now-standard Ironman distances were first established. The name of the event once again came from Collins himself, who famously said "Whoever finishes first, we'll call him the Iron Man."

On February 18, 1978, fifteen athletes took to the starting line and embarked on a race that would test them in ways that they never imagined. At the time, they had no idea that they were taking part in an event that would eventually become a worldwide phenomenon, attracting tens of thousands of competitors from across the globe each year. Most of them were just hoping to survive the insanely long course, and no one knew for sure just how much time it would take to complete the race. In fact, they didn't even know if they could finish it at all, although twelve of the athletes who started did eventually finish the course. In the end the first Ironman event was won by a man named Gordon Haller, who finished with a time of eleven hours, forty-six minutes, and fifty-eight seconds.

I was twenty-two-years old when I first learned what the Ironman was. At that point, the race had already started to gain notoriety, luring the world's top endurance athletes to Hawaii each year to take part. I wanted to be among them, so I signed up to compete in the race and set a goal for myself to finish faster that the time that Haller had posted in the inaugural edition. Eleven hours and forty-six minutes seemed like an obtainable finishing time. But because I had never raced in a competition of that distance before, or even spoke to anyone who had taken part in the Ironman, I wasn't exactly sure how well I'd perform.

Just days before the race, I flew to Hawaii and immediately after getting off the plane, I got my first taste of what I could expect from my initial Ironman experience. Several of the other athletes were at the airport waiting to collect their bags and gear. They were laughing and joking amongst themselves and I took the opportunity to size up the competition; I wasn't exactly pleased at what I saw. They all looked like supremely confident, very fit and experienced athletes, but one in particular stood out from the others. Standing there in his tank top, he looked every bit the quintessential Greek god, sculpted from marble. His blond hair and tight, lean muscles gave him the appearance of a model turned super athlete who had just walked off the beach and decided to come race with us mere mortals. Needless to say, it was quite intimidating and I immediately felt that I was in way over my head. I hadn't even left the airport yet and I was already second-guessing my decision to compete in this race.

After collecting my bags and my bike, I quietly slipped away from the boisterous group, hoping I wouldn't run into them again. But, as fate would have it, the very next day when I got in line for the mandatory gear check prior to the start of the competition, the same group of guys was standing just in front of me. I remained silent and hoped they wouldn't take much notice of me.

As I stood their listening, I couldn't help but overhear their conversation. They were talking as if they were seasoned professionals who had competed in dozens of epic endurance events all over the world. They boasted about their accomplishments and seemed unfazed by the enormity of the race that we were all about to take part in. I on the other hand could practically hear my own knees knocking together as I wondered how I could ever hope to hang with these guys out on the course.

At one point in the conversation they turned their attention to the waters just offshore. It was there that we would be swimming the first leg of the race the next day. Sizing up the surf, they were excited to see massive waves forming and immediately began chattering amongst themselves about how they couldn't wait to dive in. They speculated that since they were accustomed to dealing with those kinds of ocean conditions back home, they would have a distinct advantage over the rest of us.

I glanced out at the water myself and was immediately struck by just how big those waves truly were. I swam regularly in the pool on the Navy base preparing for the race but I never saw waves that were anything like that. The large swells were actually crashing over the sea wall! My eyes widened as I thought about plunging into those dark, intimidating waters, and swimming for 2.4 miles in such choppy conditions. *I'm way out of my league here*, I thought to myself. *I have no business being on the same course as these guys.* I just wanted to go home.

It was right about then that the blonde guy I first saw at the airport glanced back and noticed me standing there. He eyed me up and down before asking, "Are you in this race?" I said yes, just hoping he would turn around and leave me alone. "What's that?" he asked, nodding towards my bike. "It's a Motobecane," I answered a bit sheepishly yet still proud of my bike.

This brought a few laughs from the group, with the blonde Adonis saying, "You're not actually planning on riding that in the race, are you?"

At the time I owned a road bike made by a company called Motobecane USA, which cost just $109. It was all I could afford, but it was also one of my most prized possessions. I loved that bike and it had served me well both in training for, and while competing in, plenty of races.

It was about then that I noticed that my antagonist was standing beside a beautiful, high-end Bianchi bike that was fully equipped with Campagnolo Super Record components, essentially the best bike parts that money could buy. Serious triathletes will spend thousands of dollars getting their bicycles equipped and balanced just right, and clearly he had invested heavily in his ride. This was something he was extremely eager to point out by indicating that his titanium pedals alone cost more than my entire bike.

This elicited another round of laughs from the group and only served to make me more intimated. Feeling like I was in way over my head, I just wanted to slink away. The race hadn't even started yet, and I already felt like I had lost.

One of the other guys in the group told the leader to "leave the kid alone." But the surfer-boy couldn't resist taking one more jab at me as he wandered away to join his friends. "So that's a Motobecane," he said, adding a derisive "Huh" for good measure as he turned to walk away. His words would echo through my head for the next twenty-four hours. I was feeling so out of my element that I was sure that I didn't deserve to be in this race with this caliber of athletes.

When race day finally arrived I was anxious, excited, and more than a little ready to get things underway. I knew that once the starting gun went off, I'd be able to put all of the intimidation and uncertainty behind me, and just concentrate on the task at hand, which was to swim, ride, and run farther than I had ever gone before. There were still plenty of question marks in my mind, but out on the course, I knew that it would just be me chasing the macro-goals that I had set for myself. My plan was to not only finish the race but also try to beat Gordon Haller's winning time of 11:46. Everything else was just background noise.

There were 535 of us at the starting line that day and with the crack of the starting pistol we all rushed headlong into the water. The surf off the coast of Hawaii was everything I had feared when I first spotted it from the shore—big, powerful, and unpredictable. But I soon learned that I was more than up for to the task of navigating my way through those waves, completing the 2.4-mile swim course in solid fashion.

When I came out of the water, I learned that I was in 275th place, but already my confidence and mental toughness were growing. I hadn't just survived the swim, I'd felt strong out on the water, and I still had a very long bike ride and run to make up some ground. More importantly, something significant had clicked in my mind. No matter how hard it was going to be, no matter how much pain I would endure, my plan was to pass everyone who was in front of me and win the toughest race in the world. I put my head down and pedaled hard. I had 274 competitors I was determined to pass, regardless of how much pain would come my way.

By putting my head down, I assumed an aerodynamic position on my bike and concentrated on catching everyone in front of me. It wasn't long before other riders were slipping off my rear wheel, falling back as I gobbled up every other competitor in sight. I passed twenty-five riders, then fifty, then one hundred. With a renewed sense of purpose and a surge of self-confidence, I had finally started to find my rhythm. As I passed one of the riders he yelled at me and said, "don't forget you still have a marathon to run." I took that as a complement considering I had passed him with such ease.

At about the forty-five-mile point, I spotted my antagonist pedaling hard on his high-end Bianchi not far ahead of me. I was steadily gaining ground and would soon overtake him. But I knew I couldn't just let this moment pass without taking an opportunity to serve up a slice of humble pie. After all, he didn't hesitate to take shots at me—or my bike—when he was overflowing with confidence prior to the start of the race.

As I pulled up alongside of him, I glanced down at his very expensive bike and just as he realized who it was that was passing him. I simply said, "So that's a Bianchi," adding a "Huh" for good measure. With that, I put my head down again and continued pedaling hard, pulling away without ever looking back. The man who had intimidated me just a day earlier was no longer quite so terrifying. I had left him in the dust as I continued passing as many riders as I could. As a side note, I would see that same man again at the awards ceremony and he was very kind to me. I ended up beating him by over two hours.

The bike ride was far from over, and I continued to pass other riders. I had noticed a helicopter flying overhead following a rider in front of me. As I got closer to that athlete I realized it was my hero, the champion himself, Gordon Haller. I had his photo from *Sports Illustrated* hanging on my wall for over a year. I would look at it every day before my workouts, often wondering not only how a person could complete an Ironman but how a person wins an Ironman. He motivated me beyond words and he didn't even know it.

It seemed surreal to me to actually pass the original Ironman himself. As I rode around him, I gave a nod to the man who was my inspiration and said, with great respect, "Have a great race, champ." He returned the nod as I continued on my way, screaming towards the next transition area where I'd abandon my Motobecane and begin the marathon.

Soon I was off the bike and running the final stage of the Ironman. I continued to pass other competitors, and by the halfway point of the running leg I was hovering around fifieth place overall. I still had a lot of runners to catch before the finish line.

It was around that point that I heard another runner coming up behind me. I hadn't been passed yet in this race, so I was naturally curious as to who it was that was gaining ground. I glanced over my shoulder to discover Gordon Haller himself had caught up and was now matching me stride for stride. He had always been a power-ful runner and on the final stage he was kicking it hard in an effort to finish strong. Someone from the crowd yelled, "Watch out, the champion is a runner." Our final two miles were at a sub-7:30 min-ute pace.

As much as I admired and respected Haller, I wasn't about to concede the race to him just because he was my hero. As he moved to pass me, I stepped up the pace too, increasing my tempo to give chase. Back and forth we went, each pushing the other to our limits in the final miles of the race. In the end though, he was simply stron-ger than I was. Taking a short lead as we rounded our way towards the finish line he crossed just a second in front of me, and we contin-ued down the beach and splashed into the water, relief and exhaus-tion catching up with us both.

As we enjoyed the moment, Gordon came over to me and gave me a very firm hug. He thanked me for pushing him down the stretch. It had been a hell of a race, and I beamed ear-to-ear from the unexpected compliment from the original Iron Man himself. It was a classy move and truly one of the highlights of my athletic career.

I ended up finishing in thirty-eighth place overall and beat Gordon's winning time of 11:46 with a time of 11:41, far exceed-ing my own expectations. But perhaps more importantly, I had accomplished my macro-goal and gained a great deal of confidence along the way. I now knew that I could indeed hang with these top tier endurance athletes, many of whom were older, more experienced, and stronger than I was. But my ability to push through my own personal boundaries and remain mentally strong throughout a difficult race helped to level the playing field tremendously.

True to form, completing this race in Hawaii served as a springboard to launch other macro-goals. It was what led me to attempt a Double Iron Triathlon, pushing myself even further and harder. Years later I would actually become the owner and race director of that event, fulfilling yet another goal.

I had learned how to tame the physical challenges while remaining focused and mentally tough no matter the conditions. I knew that if I kept my head down and continued to move forward, I could accomplish great things, both as an athlete and as a Navy SEAL. Later, I would learn to channel those same tactics to business and life in general.

Considering my early background with motorcycles and motocross racing, it probably comes as no surprise that one of my biggest heroes growing up was Evel Knievel. Born Robert Craig Knievel, Jr., his life followed a similar trajectory as my own. At a young age he had several run-ins with the law and found himself in jail on more than one occasion. It was a police officer that first gave him the moniker "Evil," rhyming it with Knievel's last name. Later he would change the spelling however, saying he didn't want to be associated with anything that was "evil."

With his life going nowhere fast, Knievel knew he had to get his act together, so he joined the military and served a brief stint in the US Army. Much like it did for me, this experience helped to bring some much-needed discipline to his life. After completing his service, he returned home to Butte, Montana where he played semi-pro hockey, worked odd jobs, and took up ski jumping.

Not long after that he would marry his high school sweetheart and the two would have their first child. It was then that Knievel knew he had to find a way to support his family, so he worked for a time as a hunting guide, and joined the motocross circuit, before eventually embarking on a career as an insurance salesman. Later, Evel started selling motorcycles and in an effort to drum up business he would perform stunts on the bikes. It wasn't long before he was riding wheelies in the parking lot and jumping over parked cars, much to the thrill and amazement of bystanders. He quickly discovered that people would pay good money to watch him do tricks, which eventually led to the idea of starting his own traveling show. Over time, his stunts would become more and more daring—not to mention dangerous—skyrocketing him to fame and fortune. It wasn't long before fans started flocking to sold-out shows to watch Knievel jump over an ever-increasing number of cars. Some even came simply to witness one of his equally-famous crashes.

Knievel's most famous jumps included an attempt to clear the fountain outside Caesars Palace in Las Vegas and to cross the Snake River Canyon in Idaho. Both of those ended in utter failure, complete with spectacular crashes. This has led many people to remember Evel Knievel more for his failures rather than his successes. But Evel was a master at learning from both his triumphs and missteps, finding ways to improve his performance in an effort to please his adoring fans and draw an even bigger crowd.

Evel once said, "A man can fall many times in life, but he's never a failure until he refuses to get back up." That pretty much sums up his life, as the daredevil met with plenty of failure along the way, and yet managed to rise to such heights of stardom that he was recognized the world over.

At various times in his career, Knievel held a number of Guinness World Records, including the record for most bones broken in a lifetime. But perhaps his crowning achievement came in 1973 at the Los Angeles Coliseum where he managed to jump more than fifty cars, setting a record that would stand for thirty-five years. In order to do that succesfully, he had to continually examine the things that he had done well on previous jumps while simultaneously looking for ways to get just a little more performance out of both his body and his bike.

An eternal optimist, Knievel never stopped believing in himself, no matter how big of a challenge he set for his next stunt. Most of us could learn a thing or two from his determination, focus, and complete lack of fear. More often than not those are the traits that are in short supply when we are pursuing our own goals, and which sometimes keep us from achieving all that we set out to do. That wasn't a problem for Evel, who never lacked for self-confidence.

At various points in his career he was not just the star of the show, but also his own promotor, ticket salesman, truck driver, stunt coordinator, and master of ceremonies. Through it all, he worked hard, never lost sight of his goals, and was a shameless self-promotor, all of which would ultimately contribute to his massive success. He was so much more than just a daredevil. He was a businessman, a showman, and a visionary all rolled into one.

It is easy to focus on Evel's failures, but the vast majority of his stunts were major successes as he completed more than three hundred jumps throughout his long career. At one point he had gotten so good at his craft and had such a thorough understanding of what he needed to do in order to be successful, that he didn't even bother to install a speedometer on his motorcycle. He trusted his own skill, knowledge, and instincts completely, and usually those instincts were completely right.

I've always admired Evel, both as a daredevil and businessman. Not only was he an extreme athlete long before that term even existed, he was also able to turn his self-made brand into a worldwide phenomenon, selling more than $350 million in toys, t-shirts, and other merchandise. And when ABC turned down a contract to film his jump over the fountain at Caesars Palace, Knievel hired someone to film it for him, then sold that footage to the TV network for more money than he had initially asked for. He was tough, savvy, and confident which is probably why he was such an American success story.

Sometimes the path from past successes to future accomplishments isn't quite as linear as we'd like, particularly if the next macrogoal that you've set for yourself is something that no one has ever done before. But what happens when you set out to do something incredibly grand, only to have someone else beat you to the punch? Do you choose to just give up on the goal altogether, or do you go searching for another one instead?

That is exactly the dilemma that Norwegian explorer Roald Amundsen faced at one point in his illustrious career. In the early twentieth century, Amundsen was among just a handful of men who had helped chart the remote and dangerous polar regions of our planet, filling in some of the final blank spots on the map.

In 1903, he and a small crew set out to become the first men to successfully navigate the Northwest Passage, a waterway that flows through the Arctic above northern Canada, connecting the Atlantic Ocean with the Pacific. Today, thanks to climate change, this waterway is a navigable route that is used by commercial and private shipping traffic during the warmer months of the year. But in the days of Amundsen, it was little more than a myth that promised a faster—and potentially more profitable—way to sail from Europe to Asia.

Over the years whole expeditions had disappeared searching for the Northwest Passage, but Amundsen and his team actually managed a successful crossing, reaching the Pacific almost three years after they first set out. It was a historic moment in polar exploration, demonstrating that prolonged expeditions could be successful, even in the harshest of conditions.

While traveling through the Arctic, Amundsen and his crew spent long periods of time living with the local Inuit tribes who taught them how to survive in the frigid north. These indigenous people taught the Europeans how to make igloos to serve as shelter from the cold. They also showed them how to hunt the local wildlife and turn their furs into warm layers for protection from the harsh weather. They even taught them how to properly drive a dog sled team, providing all of the basic skills necessary to survive in one of the most demanding environments on the planet.

After completing the Northwest Passage expedition, Amundsen returned home to Norway, where he was welcomed as a hero. But not long after his return he started planning his next major undertaking. His goal was to become the first person to reach the North Pole, and he immediately set about making plans to achieve that massive task.

If he was going to be successful, Amundsen knew he needed a good crew around him, a sturdy ship to carry them as far north as possible, and plenty of equipment and supplies to help them reach the very top of the world. Most of all, he needed money to make this dream a reality.

Amundsen told potential investors that with the skills he had learned from the Inuit people, his success was assured. He would use all of the knowledge that they had imparted to him to go further north than anyone else had gone before. He was sure that he could reach the North Pole, and plant the Norwegian flag there, claiming a great victory for his country.

Unfortunately, the Norwegian explorer's North Pole expedition never got off the ground. While he was busy raising funds and planning for the journey, he received word that Americans Frederick Cook and Robert Peary both claimed to have reached the Pole on two separate expeditions. Those claims would later be called into question, but at the time Amundsen thought that he had lost the race before he even left the starting gate, beaten by rivals he hadn't even known were chasing the same prize.

Undaunted, Amundsen wasn't quite ready to give up on his dream of making exploration history. The Americans may have beaten him to the North Pole, but the South Pole had yet to be visited by any human. British explorer Robert Falcon Scott had already launched an expedition to become the first man to reach 90°S, and he had a head start on Amundsen and his men. Despite that, however, the Norwegian wasn't about to concede defeat without first putting up a fight.

Armed with all of his experience in the Arctic, not to mention the skills he had learned from the Inuit people, Amundsen took his ship and crew south to Antarctica. Scott may have had a lead on him, but the Norwegian knew that his team was better prepared to deal with the conditions they would face on the frozen continent. He also knew that the weather there was wildly unpredictable and could easily nullify any advantage that Scott may have over him.

It turns out, Scott did indeed face a number of delays and unforeseen logistical challenges, including having his ship, the *Terra Nova*, stuck in pack ice for twenty days. As a result, Amundsen was able to close the gap on the British squad and actually began his march to the South Pole nearly two weeks ahead of his rivals.

Out on the ice, the difference between the two competing expeditions became evident. While Scott and his men wore the woolen clothing that was commonly used by polar explorers during that era, Amundsen and his crew were outfitted with thick furs better suited for keeping them warm in the frigid conditions. And while the British expedition used small ponies to carry their gear and supplies, Amundsen's group took trained sled dog teams and were equipped with skis rather than marching on foot. This allowed them to move faster and more efficiently across the frozen plains, just as the Norwegian had predicted.

On December 14, 1911, Amundsen and four of his men completed their Antarctic crossing, reaching the South Pole ahead of Scott's team. In fact, it would be another month before the British would arrive at that same point, finding a small tent, a Norwegian flag, and a note from the rival team awaiting him. Sadly, the Brits would suffer a number of setbacks on their return trip, with the entire expedition eventually perishing out on the ice. Robert Falcon Scott and his crew remain some of the most tragic figures in the history of exploration more than a century after their deaths.

In contrast, Amundsen and his men returned home as heroes once again. They had achieved everything they had set out to do, and thanks to careful planning, meticulous preparation, and use of the knowledge they had gained in the Arctic, the expedition went off relatively problem free. The Norwegian explorer would later go on to reach the North Pole as well, becoming the first person in history to visit the two most extreme points on our planet.

It would have been easy for Amundsen to give up on his dream of trying to make exploration history. He lost the race to the North Pole to the Americans, and with a British rival already en route to the South Pole, he could have simply decided to stay home and rest on the laurels of his already impressive achievements. But, he hadn't accomplished everything that he had set out to do just yet, which only fueled his passion to pursue his goals. In the end, he would go on to become arguably the greatest polar explorer in history, spending many more years charting the frigid corners of our planet.

Amundsen's competitors were smart, talented, and driven men

in their own right, but the things that allowed him to succeed where others had failed were his adaptability and willingness to continue to learn new things. His early forays into the Arctic brought him in close contact with the people who had lived in those harsh environments for centuries, and he knew that by adopting some of their techniques he had a much higher chance of success and survival. That proved crucial to his success while navigating the Northwest Passage, but more importantly, the things he learned on that journey eventually allowed him to reach the South Pole, too.

Most of us won't end up pursuing goals quite as lofty as Amundsen's, but there is still a lot that we can learn from him. It is easy to admire his adaptability and determination, but ultimately it was his ability to take the knowledge that he had gained on his previous expeditions and apply it to future endeavors that truly set him apart from his contemporaries. This allowed him to achieve things that no one else had, while also assuring him a place in the history books. Today, he is still revered for his accomplishments, and a research station located at the South Pole bears both his name and that of Robert Falcon Scott.

Amundsen wasn't the only Norwegian explorer who had a knack for learning from his previous successes. In 1947, anthropologist Thor Heyerdahl famously sailed a homemade raft of Polynesian design called the *Kon-Tiki* for 5,000 miles across the Pacific Ocean. His goal was to prove that the islands of the South Pacific could have been first settled by travelers coming from South America, which most thought impossible at the time. When his book about the voyage was released, it became an instant bestseller across the globe and was eventually translated into seventy different languages, making Heyerdahl a household name. Later, a documentary film produced about the *Kon-Tiki* expedition went on to win the Academy Award for Best Documentary Feature.

What most people don't know is that they voyage of the *Kon-Tiki* was only Heyerdahl's first expedition by raft. In 1969, he undertook another long distance voyage, this time on a boat made of papyrus in the fashion of ancient Egyptian vessels. That raft was called the *Ra* and it was built to attempt a crossing of the Atlantic Ocean starting in Morocco. Partway through the trip however, the *Ra* began to take on water and the mission had to be abandoned.

Later, Heyerdahl and his team discovered that they had missed an important step in their boat-building process and corrected it in a second version dubbed the *Ra II*. In 1970, the new raft shoved off once again, and this time it sailed successfully across the Atlantic, pushed along by the Canary Current until it arrived in Barbados. The Norwegian had once again proven that ancient people could have sailed vast distances across hostile oceans using rudimentary vessels.

Still not content with his seafaring adventures, Heyerdahl returned to the ocean in 1977 in another vessel built from papyrus called the *Tigris*. This time the plan was to prove that ancient sailors from Mesopotamia could have sailed all the way to Southeast Asia to open trade routes with that part of the world. The ship was still seaworthy and making steady progress towards its goal five months after setting out. But later it was deliberately burned by its crew to protest ongoing military conflicts in the Middle East, bringing an abrupt halt to the expedition. Up until that point, it appeared that Heyerdahl might once again prove that civilizations from the distant past were capable of traveling further and faster than we had ever thought possible before.

When the Norwegian set out on his first journey aboard the *Kon-Tiki*, he wasn't sure if he could actually survive at sea for weeks on end. His theories were unproven and generally scoffed at, as no one at the time believed it was possible for humans to sail on a primitive craft for thousands of miles across a hostile ocean. Heyerdahl proved that his ideas weren't just a possibility, they were a reality, and in the process he changed the way we looked at our world and how we explored it. His success wasn't just groundbreaking—it was paradigm-shifting.

Later, the anthropologist and adventurer took all of the knowledge that he had gained aboard the *Kon-Tiki* and applied it to his other sailing expeditions. He now knew what it would take to survive at sea for a prolonged period of time and that directly contributed to his success on the *Ra II* in particular, and to a lesser extent, the *Tigris*, as well.

There is an old saying that says "success breeds success," which essentially means that once someone has been successful in some sort of venture, they usually tend to be successful in achieving other goals, too. Confidence generated from achieving our objectives plays a significant role in this process of course, but another significant part of the equation is the knowledge that is gained along the way. When you combine the things you learned with the confidence that is gained, you get a powerful mixture indeed.

Former Apple CEO Steve Jobs, a guy who knew a thing or two about success, was fond of saying "Those who are crazy enough to think they can change the world usually do." The real tragedy isn't that people or organizations set their goals too high and never reach them, it is that they set them too low and do achieve them. You'll never learn anything from those types of success and it isn't exactly a way to change the world, now is it?

I believe that learning from past success plays an important role in future successes too. When you reach the macro-goals that you've set for yourself, by all means take some time to revel in the accomplishment—you deserve it! But when you've finished patting yourself on the back, be sure to also take some time to examine the things that went right with the process. Chances are, you'll discover plenty of experiences that can be applied to your next project as well, providing a template that can lead to even more amazing things.

BILL GATES
Philanthropist

There was a time when labeling Microsoft co-founder Bill Gates as anything other than a businessman or entrepreneur would have seemed strange. For the first half of his career he was best known for creating a company that has helped shape the way we use technology in the modern age and created a software platform that is run on 90 percent of the personal computers in the world. That made Gates a billionaire many times over and turned him into one of the true luminaries of the computer revolution. But for his second act, he's set even loftier goals for himself and in the process he could potentially save the lives of millions of people across the globe.

Born in Seattle, Washington, in 1955, William Henry Gates was always a bright student who took an interest in technology. He wrote his first computer program when he was just thirteen years old, at a time when computers filled rooms and didn't yet sit comfortably on the top of a desk. When he graduated high school in 1973 he was recognized as a National Merit Scholar, scored a 1590 (out of 1600) on his SAT, and was accepted at Harvard, where he majored in pre-law.

It wasn't long before Gates started taking computer science and mathematics classes instead and was writing impressive, efficient programming code. That earned him notoriety with the faculty and other students, who were impressed with his problem solving skills. It also earned him a summer job at Honeywell in 1974, where he reconnected with boyhood friend Paul Allen. The two young men ended up starting their own software company that same year, calling their start-up Microsoft. Gates would never return to Harvard after that.

Microsoft began its life by creating a software language interpreter that was used to create BASIC programs in the early days of microcomputers. But later they would connect with IBM who was looking for an operating system to run on its soon-to-be-launched line of personal computers. Gates and Allen secured such an OS for IBM and MS-DOS was born.

Shrewdly, Gates and Allen did not sell MS-DOS to IBM, but chose to license it to the PC maker instead. This allowed them to do the same with other companies as well and before long MS-DOS was being installed on thousands of computers. Eventually, Microsoft would also introduce the Windows operating system as well, which ran on the DOS platform. Windows provided a graphical interface that allowed non-technical computer users to more easily work with their PCs. Over time, and with the growth of the Internet, Windows grew into a smash hit that spawned numerous iterations, turning Microsoft into the driving force in the computer industry throughout the 1990s and early 2000s.

The success of Windows also made Gates the richest man in the world, with an estimated worth of more than $90 billion. But all of that money was just a large number on a spreadsheet for most of his career as he chose to stay focused on running Microsoft. It wasn't until he met his future-wife Melinda French in 1994 that he started to explore life outside of the company. She is the one who is credited for turning Bill's attention to other aspects of life, and convincing him to start thinking about all the ways his vast wealth could be used for good.

In 2000, the duo created the Bill and Melinda Gates Foundation, which started with an endowment of more than $5 billion. Since then, the nonprofit has only grown in size and reach. Additionally, the couple have also announced plans to give away 95 percent of their wealth to help fund a variety of programs. With those kinds of resources available to them, the Gates family can set their sights on accomplishing some pretty impressive goals, which is exactly what they've done.

The Gates Foundation's stated agenda is to stamp out poverty around the globe. That's a pretty tall order, even for someone as smart, well-connected, and wealthy as Bill Gates. Still, you have to admire anyone who looks for massive goals to tackle and ways to achieve them. In this case, Gates and his organization are working with the governments of developing countries, large non-governmental organizations, a variety of corporations, and other philanthropists on plans to improve the lives of millions round the world.

Ending world poverty isn't the only major goal on Gates's list however. He has also stated that he is committed to finding a cure for malaria, a waterborne disease that kills hundreds of thousands on an annual basis. Stamping out this disease will be no small task, but Bill has committed more than $1 billion to doing just that. He has made it his goal to help find a cure by 2040, using a mix of science and technology to achieve that objective.

While malaria may be Gates's most well-known fight against disease, he has also said that he is committed to stamping out polio and fighting Alzheimer's as well. He's also helped fund research on a new type of rice that is genetically modified to fight vitamin A deficiencies, while also supporting efforts to provide improved educational opportunities both in the US and abroad. His goals, much like his philanthropic work, are far reaching.

Is achieving some of these goals a real long shot? Probably. But Gates believes that they are worth pursuing nonetheless. If he doesn't at least try, perhaps no one else will either. Few persons on the planet have as many resources at their disposal, which is why Gates's commitment to these causes is so exciting. Those resources could be a true game changer, which is the reason the Microsoft co-founder has set such lofty goals for himself and his foundation.

Bill Gates has always been a dreamer. When he and Paul Allen founded Microsoft, their hope was to provide tools that would make it easier for people to use their computers. Over time, they were able to do just that, helping to fuel a technology revolution that has changed the way we work, play, and communicate with one another. The software that they created has had a profound effect on the modern world and that alone would be a worthy legacy for most people.

But after building a software empire, Gates turned his attention on even more pressing matters for much of the world's population. He's hoping to improve the health of billions. He wants to help educate the next generation of thinkers, and he wants to leave a lasting mark on our planet that goes far beyond the technology space. If he succeeds, future generations may not remember Gates as the many who created the Windows operating system, but will instead remember him in the same breath as Andrew Carnegie and John D. Rockefeller, great philanthropists who took their vast wealth and used it to make the world a better place. That's exactly what Gates is hoping to do too, and considering his impressive track record, I wouldn't bet against him succeeding in this arena too.

Chapter 6

WHAT NAVY SEAL TRAINING TAUGHT ME

"Success breeds complacency. Complacency breeds failure."
—Andy Grove

One of the most important lessons that I learned when I began to find some success as an athlete is that if I pushed myself hard enough, I could actually succeed in accomplishing things I felt were quite significant. This led to me training even harder as a runner, eventually achieving my goal of finishing a marathon in under two hours and fifty minutes. It was about that same time that I began to think about what else I could do with my life. I found myself wanting to do something worthwhile. Something that would allow me to channel all of the energy that I had built up in a positive way. I wanted to go somewhere that I could make a difference. I found everything I was looking for—and so much more—in the US Navy.

Not long after I enlisted in the military I found myself in Great Lakes, Illinois where I underwent basic training. At the time, I wasn't sure what to expect from this new life, but it didn't take long before I started to feel right at home. The regimented nature of the Navy brought some much-needed order and structure to my life and soon I was making sense of the predictable routine. And since I was already in fairly good physical condition, it wasn't long before I began to thrive in this new environment.

Unlike Marine Boot Camp, Navy Boot Camp is not especially physically challenging for someone who is in decent shape. I knew that in order to stay fit, and continue to become even fitter, I needed to do additional training after hours. So as soon as the drill instructors left us alone in the evenings, I made excellent use of that time. Instead of shining my shoes, folding my clothes or studying the *Navy Blue Jacket Manual* as the other recruits did, I set a goal of doing a thousand repetitions of various exercises each night. One night it was a thousand push-ups, one night it would be a thousand bunkbed bench presses, one night it would be a thousand sit ups, and so on. After my nightly strength training, I would run laps in the barracks, around all of the bunk beds. One time I ran seventeen miles in the barracks, over one hundred laps. I did this seven nights a week for two months. The boot camp company officer noticed my commitment to working out and selected me to be the physical fitness instructor which meant one of my boot camp duties was to assist other recruits who were having difficulties with the physical requirement. I gladly and proudly accepted this new role as it gave me the opportunity to help others and to continue my own training as well. It was perfect.

One day, after we had completed a training session in the swimming pool, one of our drill instructors asked if any of us recruits wanted to watch a film about the Navy SEALs. At the time, none of knew much, if anything, about the SEALs, but some of us were more than intrigued. I didn't know it just yet, but that day would end up changing the course of my life forever, sending me down a career path that I had never imagined for myself.

While the SEALs can trace their origins back to the Amphibious Scouts and Raiders of World War II, they were first formed by a presidential directive in the early 1960s. John F. Kennedy recognized the need for a highly trained counter-guerilla unit to serve as the tip of the spear in Southeast Asia and wanted a new type of warrior to fill the role. This unit would be able to operate from the sea, land, and air, hence the SEAL acronym.

The first SEAL teams were formed in early 1962, with SEAL Team One located at the Coronado Naval Base in Coronado, California and SEAL Team Two in Little Creek, Virginia. The members of those two units were selected from the Navy's Underwater Demolition Teams, which had already conducted commando style raids and missions throughout the Korean War. Their mission was to conduct counter guerrilla warfare and clandestine operations anywhere in the world.

While the Underwater Demolition Teams were already highly skilled at their craft, the newly christened SEALs immediately began an intensive training program that focused on hand-to-hand combat, high-altitude skydiving, demolitions, and maritime raids. They also studied foreign languages, small unit tactics, and became experts at the use of a variety of firearms.

SEALs did conduct reconnaissance operations in Cuba, but they found their first real challenge in Vietnam where they were sent to serve as advisors and trainers. They helped prepare South Vietnamese forces to combat communist insurgents from the North, using many of the same weapons, tactics, techniques, and procedures that the SEAL teams were using themselves.

Over the course of the Vietnam War, the SEALs proved highly efficient, carrying out some of the most daring and dangerous missions assigned to US forces as a part of that conflict. They not only trained Vietnamese troops and served as advisors in the south, but conducted raids into North Vietnam, Laos, and Cambodia, quickly becoming one of the most reliable and feared units in the US military.

In the early 1980s additional SEAL teams were commissioned, giving the Navy greater flexibility in when and where the elite units could be deployed. As a result, SEALs have operated in places like Grenada, Panama, Somalia, the Philippines, El Salvador, Iraq, and Afghanistan. They've also conducted missions in other parts of the world, usually under a deep veil of secrecy.

Today, the Navy SEALs are considered the toughest, most experienced, and best-trained combat units in the world. They are elite warriors who are assigned some of the most challenging operations that the US military conducts, and more often than not they successfully complete those tasks without anyone ever knowing about their accomplishments. They undertake these dangerous missions not for fame, fortune, or glory, but because they've made an oath to protect their country.

After learning what SEALs do and how they train, I had one massive macro-goal in life; that was to join their ranks as soon as possible. I had never wanted anything else quite so much and all of my focus and time was devoted to becoming fitter, stronger, faster, and more knowledgeable of how the SEALs operated. I knew the training would be tough but I was ready to welcome the pain!

I immediately requested permission to be assigned to BUD/S (Basic Underwater Demolition/SEAL) training after I completed boot camp and hospital corpsman training. But even though I met all of the physical requirements, my request was denied. The SEALs didn't want a raw recruit. Instead, they were looking for corpsman who had field experience in saving lives and treating the wounded. So this meant I need to be assigned to a unit where I could gain some experience first.

Following corpsman training I was assigned to the Naval Regional Medical Center in Newport, Rhode Island, where I gained valuable on-the-job training working in the ER and ICU. As my time in Newport was coming to a close, I was getting more and more excited about receiving my orders for BUD/S. But before that happened I was given more bad news. The Navy had passed a new policy requiring all Navy corpsman to choose to serve either with the Marines or accept shipboard duty instead. I didn't want to do either of those things, and once again reiterated my desire to go to BUD/S. I was told in no uncertain terms that I didn't have a choice in the matter, and I had to pick between either the Marines or a ship. Reluctantly, I chose the Marines Corps, and was assigned to Camp Pendleton, California, which happened to be located just up the road from where the SEALs trained in Coronado.

Since I was stationed in Newport, Rhode Island and was being transferred to the West Coast, I was given ten days travel time. I thought that in ten days, I could ride my bicycle from Rhode Island to California no problem. After doing some quick math, I determined I would need to peddle three hundred miles a day and in ten days, I would have a 3,000-mile ride completed and would still be on time to check in at my new duty station. Simple as could be. I planned on doing the ride with a friend of my family, but before we even got to the half way point, he quit on me. We packed up the bikes and finished our cross-country ride in a station wagon. I always thought that I would attempt the ride alone at a later date at some point. It never happened, a regret I will have for the rest of my life.

Soon after we completed our cross-country journey, I checked into the Marine Base at Camp Pendleton and immediately drove down to Coronado to speak directly with the Master Chief of SEAL Team One. I explained my situation, and told him that I that I didn't want to be assigned to the Marines. I told him that I wanted to receive orders for BUD/S instead. He informed me that although the Teams desperately needed good corpsmen, before I could be assigned to BUD/S I'd first have to complete the five week field medical course with the Marine Corps.

My five weeks of training buzzed by and I graduated top of the class, which brought a great sense of pride and accomplishment. But when I requested orders to start BUD/S yet again, I was then told that the Marine's hadn't invested all of the time and effort in training me, just to lose me to the SEALs afterwards. My new orders said that I had to deploy with the Marines first. So, once again, I packed my bags, this time heading to Okinawa, Japan for my thirteen-month assignment.

While in Okinawa, I gained some outstanding experience as a field corpsman, treating Marines for all types of injuries. I also had the chance to travel around the world to compete in various endurance competitions. My Marine Corps chain of command was thrilled to have an athlete assigned to them who was competing— and often placing high—in marathons, bicycle races, and triathlons.

My tour with the Marines in Okinawa turned out to be a highly positive one, and I ended up enjoying it more than I ever imagined. Despite that however, I never once gave up on my ultimate goal of becoming a SEAL. I categorized every race I competed in as a micro-goal with the macro-goal still squarely focused on graduating from BUD/S.

Eventually I was sent back stateside and ended up serving with a Navy Reserve unit stationed in Pennsylvania. After that, I worked for a short time as a prison guard, until one day I finally received the orders I had been waiting for. I was told to report to BUD/S in the next thirty days.

It was one of the happiest moments of my life.

What followed was months of grueling physical and mental challenges that were not only designed to help my classmates and I be as prepared as possible, but also turn us into the most disciplined and well-trained warriors on the planet. We honed our skills at combat, swimming and diving, shooting, demolition training, small unit tactics, and maritime operations. We also learned how to function as a well-organized team—both in and out of the water—practicing hand-to-hand and small arms tactics along the way. We learned to navigate using a map and compass, practiced rappelling, and became proficient in using demolitions like C4 and TNT to destroy underwater targets. It was both exhausting and exhilarating at the same time, and when it was over, our class of 108 had been whittled down to just twenty-three men who had survived the intense experience.

Even after completing the arduous training, I still wasn't technically a Navy SEAL. A six-month probation period followed, which included additional advanced training in a wide variety of areas. I attended and truly enjoyed the survival, evasion, resistance escape (SERE) training. I graduated as an honor student and was asked to raise the American flag when the course ended. I also became more skilled as a corpsman by attending a two-month long Special Forces Medic course, and earned my static line and free fall jump certifications. Although I had achieved my goal of graduating from BUD/S, I didn't spend a whole lot of time patting myself on the back. Instead I continued to learn new skills, many of which would come in very handy in the years that followed.

Eventually I did earn my SEAL Trident, however, launching what would become an eighteen-year career as part of the Navy's elite commando unit. In the years that followed, I was lucky enough to serve with some incredibly professional and dedicated men who ultimately helped shape the person that I would become. Time and again we put our lives into each other's hands as we conducted missions in places like El Salvador, Panama, Afghanistan, and Iraq.

We often ended up going through hell together, but ultimately that helped galvanize us as a unit and as friends.

Over the course of my time as a SEAL, I learned a great deal about how to achieve great things while testing and pushing my own limits in ways I'd never imagined. Most of those lessons had at least as much to do with being mentally tough, focused, and determined, as they did about being strong, agile, and fit. I've often said that our training was 90 percent mental and 10 percent physical, and I've found that tends to hold true for just about anything you want to achieve in life, whether it is competing in a ten-day adventure race, climbing a mountain or finding success in business.

SEALs have a motto that says "the only easy day was yesterday." This saying isn't just a reflection of the intense training and preparation that a SEAL goes through but is practically a way of life for the men on the Teams. Basically, it means that in order to keep sharpening your skills, improving your performance, and inching towards your objectives and goals, you have to work harder today than you did yesterday. This is a philosophy that any SEAL trainee has to embrace when he enters BUD/S, and it continues to play an important role throughout the length of his career.

This is a mantra that has served me well both in and out of the military. As a SEAL, it drove me to become the best individual and teammate that I could possibly be, spurred on by the knowledge that my actions could have life or death consequences for myself or my teammates. In the world of covert actions, counter-terrorism, and guerrilla warfare, there is very little room for error, which is why we trained at such a high level all of the time. Standing still was simply not an option, which meant that finding new and creative ways to improve our skillsets was a vital component of what we did.

Endurance athletes are no strangers to hard work either, and the idea of continually pushing the envelope helped me to achieve big things in the marathons, triathlons, adventure races, and other events. In almost all cases, there were other athletes who were faster, stronger, smarter, and more experienced than I was, giving them a physical advantage that isn't easy to overcome. But, I believe that very few of those men and women actually worked harder than I did. That, coupled with a tough mindset and a fierce desire to win, allowed me to compete with people who were superior athletes, but lacked the unrelenting drive and passion to truly achieve greatness.

When it comes to pursuing our own personal goals, the idea that each day will be more challenging than the last is a good way to remind ourselves that there are always new challenges on the horizon. We can't be sure what form those challenges will take, but by working hard and preparing to the best of our abilities, we'll be better equipped to deal with them when they arrive.

Another important lesson that I learned while serving with the SEALs is that there are actually two types of pain: the temporary pain you'll feel while training and the permanent pain of regret that comes from not achieving the things that you envision for yourself. I didn't mind the former and actually welcomed the pain as part of the learning process. Although, I do have a few regrets in my life, I have always tried to limit them as much as possible. There is no worse feeling than not achieving the things that I'd set out to do.

Essentially, if you want to achieve anything in life, you'll have to work hard, test yourself both mentally and physically, and step outside of your comfort zone from time to time. Along the way, there will probably be times when you'll feel uncomfortable as you deal with stress, uncertainty, and exhaustion. But none of those feelings last forever and when you eventually achieve whatever it is you're striving for, all of the pain and sacrifice that it took to get you there will soon fade into a distant memory.

On the other hand, if you sit on the sidelines waiting for the right time to go after that goal, chances are you'll miss your window of opportunity. Anything that is worth achieving comes with a certain amount of risk, and that can sometimes paralyze us into inaction. If that happens, you'll more than likely eventually end up regretting those missed opportunities. That is a feeling that can linger for a very long time, possibly even haunting you for the rest of your life.

In our ongoing analogy of the person who wants to run a marathon, the pain that comes with training is very real and tangible. Tired legs, pulled muscles, and sore feet are all par for the course when preparing to compete in such a lengthy race. But when all of that training and preparation is completed, and race day finally arrives, the long weeks of hard work will eventually pay off. The sense of pride and accomplishment that comes with having completed the marathon will make all of the miles spent out on the road seem well worth it. Hopefully you will even start thinking about the next challenge before you've even fully recovered from your previous event.

Compare that to the feelings of regret that someone might have when they've always had a dream but have never had the courage or conviction to pursue it. Whether it's running a marathon, starting your own business, traveling to a foreign country, or whatever else you might be passionate about, don't be afraid to get off the couch and go for it. In the long run, you won't ever regret the hard work, planning, and dedication required to achieve that dream, even if you fail. At least you'll know that you gave it a shot, which is far more rewarding than never trying at all.

During our "drown proof" training at BUD/S, I distinctly remember one of our instructors telling us that the weak amongst us would be the first to quit once the shooting started. None of us wanted to be that guy and we looked around sheepishly at each other as we considered which of us fit that description. The last thing we needed when conducting operations in the field were people who might crack under pressure. There simply isn't room for individuals who do not give there all in this line of work.

That was another lesson that has stuck with me for a lifetime and has saved my life on numerous occasions. On a SEAL team, you need to be surrounded by men that you can trust, who know how to do their job well, and who won't hesitate for a second when things start to get hairy. More importantly, the individuals who make up the team have gone to great lengths to earn a spot there, proving that they can work closely with those around them. Knowing that the man next to you won't quit, regardless of the circumstances, makes all the difference in the world.

Even though most people won't find themselves in a situation where they are getting shot at, the lesson remains the same: collaborate with competent, talented, and driven people, and you're much more likely to succeed in reaching your goals. With a solid team around you, you will accomplish more than you could on your own, which is why it is vitally important that you select good people to be a part of any of your important endeavors.

If you're building a business that typically means that you're also partnering with individuals who will not only bring something meaningful to the table but are also dedicated to helping you achieve your goals. The last thing you need is for someone that you depend upon to quit on you when things start to get tough. Setbacks are a natural part of the process, but those who lack confidence and commitment will look for a reason to bow out when things don't go their way.

It's common knowledge that Apple Computers was founded in a garage in Palo Alto, California by Steve Jobs and Steve Wozniak. The two men have become household names thanks to the iconic product the company has developed over the past four decades. From the Apple computer to the iPod to the iPhone, it is safe to say that Apple has captured lightning in a bottle on more than one occasion, growing into the most valuable company in the world in the process.

But what most people don't know is that there was a third man listed on Apple's original articles of incorporation that were drafted in 1976. That man was Ronald Wayne, who worked with Jobs and Wozniak on the original Apple computer. By all accounts, Wayne was smart and affable, and is credited with writing the user manuals for the Apple I and designing the company's first logo.

When the trio made their partnership deal Jobs and Wozniak each received 45 percent ownership in Apple in large part because they had been developing the company's first computer for months. That left a 10 percent ownership for Wayne, who was brought on to the team a bit later to offer wisdom and guidance to his partners, both of whom were twenty years his junior. But just twelve days after Apple officially became a corporation, Wayne sold his stock in the company for a mere $800, possibly making one of the biggest blunders in business history.

Why would Wayne make such a move less than two weeks after he had joined the company? Simply put, he lacked faith in the future of Apple and the men that he was working with, which in turn led to a lack of commitment to the project.

In the early days of Apple the company received an order for one hundred Apple I computers from a local electronics shop and in order to meet that demand, Jobs took out a loan for $15,000. That seemed like an exorbitant sum of money to Wayne, who feared he would be the one on the hook for the cash if the business failed. So, in order to avoid putting himself at risk, he had his co-founders pull his name off the contract and sold his shares back to them. As we all know however, Apple didn't fail and now Wayne's stake in the company would be worth tens of billions of dollars.

Of course, it is easy to look back at this move now and realize that it was a mistake to bail out when he did—hindsight is always 20/20. But by exiting Apple just a few days into the company's life, Wayne showed that he wasn't committed to the vision that Jobs and Wozniak had created. In this case, the shooting hadn't even started yet and he was already quitting. That is definitely not the kind of person you want on your team.

SEALs live by the motto "train as you fight, fight as you train." This means that in order to be completely ready for whatever comes your way in the field, you should be constantly honing your skills and preparing for any number of scenarios you might face while on a mission. That way, when the real thing does come along, your body will instinctively know how to react without even having to think about it.

For a SEAL, training is a never-ending process since there are always new skills, tactics, and techniques to learn and perfect. The philosophy behind this is that when a situation comes along that isn't training, we'll be better prepared to handle it. In other words, if you train as you fight, you're much more likely to fight as you trained once the actual shooting starts.

This mindset can be applied to a wide variety of aspects through-out your life, no matter what it is you're trying to achieve. Most successful people also happen to be life-long learners who are al-ways acquiring new skills to help them along. Those skills could be anything from learning how to run more efficiently over longer distances, to picking a new language, or incorporating a new piece of accounting software. The point is, training and preparation is an ongoing process, and mastery can only be obtained through practice and repetition. And not all practice makes perfect. Only perfect practice makes perfect!

The "train as you fight" motto was something that I applied to my athletic career as well. When preparing for a race, I very rarely went out for a slow run, slow bike ride, or easy paddle.

Instead I usually pushed myself to the limit during most of my workouts, training at or at near-race pace, so that I'd be much better prepared to handle the faster speeds that come with race day. If you only prepare by running at half-speed, you're setting yourself up for disappointment. For me, the goal was to always try to give myself the best shot at not only finishing, but placing as close to the front as possible. In order to do that, I had to train as I raced, and vice versa.

Runners often make a distinction between a "conversational pace" and "race pace." In the former, you're able to actually hold a conversation while you run, making it a much more enjoyable experience. Race pace is more intense, focused, fast, and painful too. But that's okay, as it makes the non-painful times that much more enjoyable. As a SEAL, we did not have the luxury of training at conversational pace. It was go all out, or not at all.

No matter how much you prepare and train however, things seldom go as expected. You can create a plan of action for just about any mission, and run countless training exercises prior to launching the operation, only to have things go off the rails within the first few minutes. That is simply the nature of things, and not all variables can be accounted for nor can they be predicted. SEALs believe that you should "plan your dive and dive your plan," but it often does not work out that simply. That leads to another very important lesson that I learned from my time as a SEAL: always include contingency plans while training and remember to be flexible. You'll want to be able to roll in another direction when things truly go bad.

The best laid plans can easily come undone and quite frankly we should always expect them to. Prior to any mission we would come up with numerous contingencies, trying to consider all of the potential "what if" scenarios we could face during a mission. But even with years of experience and training there was still no way to predict everything that could potentially come our way. That meant we had to be light on our feet, quick thinking, and highly adaptable.

We'd also tell ourselves, "If you're going through hell, don't slow down. Just stay focused on the mission." The point was that things rarely went as we had hoped, but that shouldn't matter. We had a job to do and everything else was secondary. If you can keep your eyes on the prize, you'll have a much better chance at being successful.

This same attitude has served me well throughout my athletic career, too. When competing in an endurance event that goes on for hours or even days at a time, things are bound to go wrong at some point. Muscles, tendons, and ligaments are subject to damage, bikes have mechanical breakdowns, teammates collapse and take ill, and sometimes you find yourself way off course. Learning to take those things in stride is crucial to reaching your goals, because the path to success is almost never as straight and easy as we'd like to believe it will be.

I can't even begin to count the number of times that things went poorly in the middle of a training exercise or mission. Being able to stay calm and recall my training saved my life and those of my teammates on many occasions. Of course, there were also more than a few painful lessons along the way.

For instance, one time while conducting a high-altitude, high-opening (HAHO) parachute insertion, I found myself in a particularly precarious situation. With a seventy-five-pound pack strapped to my body, a helmet on my head, my weapon strapped to my side, and an oxygen tank and mask secured in place I jumped out of a perfectly good aircraft at just over 18,000 feet. I ended up having an absolutely terrible exit, flipping through the risers on my parachute as I hit the night air. The risers twisted and smashed down on my helmet causing my head to violently snap to the left, ripping the O2 mask off of my face and sending a sharp pain down my body. I saw a white flash and, in that moment, I was sure that I had broken my jaw and neck.

While there was obviously cause for concern, I had other problems to contend with as well. Thanks to my poor exit, I was falling through the pitch-black night like a rock. All I had overhead was a crumpled malfunctioning parachute that was doing nothing to slow my fall.

I had to react quickly or I would hit the ground at terminal velocity. We jokingly called this type of death, "deceleration sickness." Fortunately, we had trained for these kinds of contingencies, so I knew just what to do.

Using my right hand, I pulled the cutaway pillow and released my main parachute, which instantly shot off overhead, disappearing into the night. Then, with my left hand, I pulled the reserve chute, which mercifully deployed as expected.

With things now a bit more under control, I was able to get my O2 mask back on and suck in some oxygen. I reached for my push-to-talk comms unit to let the other SEALs on the jump know what had happened. I could see their chemical light sticks high above me. We were traveling in the same direction, but I was now thousands of feet below the rest of the team.

I wanted to give them an update on my status and tell them that I would join them as quickly as I could once we were all on the ground. But as I tried to talk, all I could manage was an unintelligible mutter. I may have been able to right my fall and avoid crashing into the ground, but there was still some other issues I needed to resolve.

When the risers on my main chute snapped my head back, they had dislocated my jaw, making it impossible to talk. As a corpsman however, I had dealt with these issues on others plenty of times before and knew exactly what to do. Applying pressure on my back-bottom teeth with my thumbs and I was able to snap my jaw back into place with a single swift firm motion. There was loud pop followed by a searing pain, but everything was back to where it needed to be. After that, I was able to radio the rest of the team to let them know I was safe and I would rendezvous with them as quickly as I could.

On another occasions I ran into a problem that nearly cost me my life. We were conducting a static ship takedown, which is an operation that tasks SEALs with approaching a vessel from under the water. The SEALs silently board the target vessel by climbing to the deck of the ship using a caving ladder and a telescopic pole, and then undertake a hostage rescue and terrorist take down. These were the kinds of missions that we trained for and conducted all of the time and we were proud of our reputation for being the absolute best in the world at conducting these types of maritime missions.

On one such training exercise we were in the middle of a night dive using oxygen tanks when things started to go bad. It is important to note that when you're breathing 100 percent pure oxygen you can only remain submerged for about four hours at a depth of thirty feet before the O_2 starts to become toxic. When you hit that four-hour mark, divers can experience convulsions and seizures that can quickly lead to death.

Our dives were always at night and the dive team all dove together, a feat which is extremely hard to do. In low- and no-light conditions and in often murky water it was difficult to see anything. Worse yet, it was practically impossible to communicate with the other SEALs using anything other than hand squeezes.

After we finally identified our target ship, we prepared to derig our gear and board the vessel. Once in position, we removed our fins, weight belts, and Dräger rebreathing units, connecting them on to the line that we had rigged under the ship. The O_2 Dräger was the preferred rebreather units for Navy SEALs because it didn't give away our position underwater. Unlike when using SCUBA gear, there are no air bubbles that rise to the surface while exhaling.

After waiting ten or fifteen minutes while breathing from my Dräger attached to the derigging line, I suddenly realized that I couldn't breathe at all. Something was wrong, and I wasn't sure what the problem was. I told myself to remain calm and methodically I began checking my equipment. We had SOPs (standard operating procedures) for most everything we did. First, I ran my hand up the inhalation hose to be sure it hadn't gotten kinked or twisted somehow. When I couldn't find any problems there, I moved on to the oxygen tank itself, thinking that perhaps the valve had somehow gotten turned off. It hadn't; it was wide open. I also double-checked that the mouth piece valve had not been inadvertently turned to the off position. These were all of the SOPs I was trained to conduct, but I still couldn't breathe!

Calmly and carefully I repeated the same procedure three times, all the while my lungs were starting to burn and my head was really hurting. I was quickly running out of time, but I wasn't any closer to getting to the bottom of the problem.

Finally I reached up to my buddy's fin and shook it. He came back down to meet me. We couldn't see each other since it was pitch dark, but when I could feel his presence, I reached out toward his face with my hand to see if I could feel for his mouthpiece. He had already derigged and did not have his Dräger on, so I was unable to buddy-breathe.

Starting to get a bit more concerned, I repeated my emergency SOPs one more time: I needed to act fast or I was going to be in real trouble. My head was pounding and my body was aching to take a breath. We had one rule of engagement and that was not to get caught on this hostage rescue mission. I was about ready to blow the entire mission because I needed to take a breath, but I wasn't about to let that happen.

To complicate things even further, the ships that we trained under were large cargo ships. As a diver, you really don't have a good idea where you are under these massive floating structures. I started to swim up to the surface, heading towards the hull of the ship where I hoped I could find a spot to catch a breath without compromising the mission. In the darkness it was impossible to see where the vessel was above me, so I just put my hand over my head as I kicked upward to avoid slamming into it.

The ship was adjacent to a large buoyant structure and there was absolutely no room for me to squeeze between the two objects. By now, my brain felt like it was being stabbed with an ice pick as my oxygen levels began to deplete. I had no other option but to ignore the pain and press on. As I was taught in BUD/S just keep kicking and don't quit. So I kicked.

It had been quite a few minutes now without breathing. My head felt like it was going to explode. It was getting colder as I kicked and

I realized I must be going deeper. I had two thoughts, aside from to keep kicking. One thought was to just take a deep breath and the pain would end. I would simply drown but I wouldn't blow the mission. My second thought was, how would they ever find my body under this huge ship. Later, I was disappointed in myself for having those thoughts because I know that was exactly how a quitter would think.

So I kicked and kicked and eventually spotted a faint light in the distance. I swam under the boat from approximately midship to bow. As I surfaced, I pulled my mask down below my chin in order to avoid giving away my position with light reflecting off the glass. I was still following standard operating procedure even then so I would avoid compromising the mission.

After regaining my composure and saying a few prayers, I swam alongside the port side of the boat and joined my teammates, who were just climbing the ladder and preparing to board the ship. As I looked back across the water, I realized that the light that I had seen was cast by the moon, and it was just pure luck that I caught a glimpse of it at all.

Later in a post mission debrief, I would learn that my rebreather had a rare malfunction that caused its inhalation hose valve to freeze shut, closing off my air supply in the process. I was extremely lucky to come out of that situation alive. Without my training, which taught me to remain calm and composed under pressure, I wouldn't have survived.

The ability to stay flexible and think on your feet is a trait that everyone should master. Whether you're caught up in a heat-of-the-moment situation like the ones I've described, or you experience something less urgent but equally important, being able to switch gears, come up with an alternate plan of action, and initiate that plan is crucial. Everyone encounters those moments at some point in their life, but those with a strong mindset who are focused on reaching their goals will learn not to freeze under pressure. Instead they'll see alternate ways of reaching their objectives even as chaos surrounds them.

In the mountaineering world there are a number of well-known

incidences where this has proven to be true, but one of the most famous took place on K2 in 1953. Located in the Karakoram Mountain
Range along the border of China and Pakistan, K2 is the second tallest mountain in the world. Although its summit sits some 777 feet
lower, K2 is far more difficult to climb than Everest. So much so in
fact that while hundreds of people reach the top of Everest in any
given year, success on K2 is much more elusive with years sometimes
passing between successful summits.

In 1953, K2 had yet to be conquered, but a team of Americans
traveled to the Karakoram to see if they could crack the secret to
reaching its incredibly difficult summit. Led by legendary climber
Charlie Houston, the expedition included mountaineers Art Gilkey,
Pete Schoening, Dee Molenaar, George Bell, Tony Streather, Bob
Bates, and Robert Craig. Each was a strong and talented climber
in his own right, but they were picked as much for their easy-going
temperament as their experience and skill. Houston knew that in
order to have a chance at success, he would need a team that could
get along well, not just climb the mountain together.

As the expedition progressed the team met with a number of setbacks including poor weather conditions that prevented them from
reaching the summit. To make matters worse, Gilkey developed
blood clots in his legs which were slowly progressing through his
bloodstream, making their way towards his lungs. The entire group
knew that in order to save his life they had to get him off the mountain as quickly as possible, so they put their sick teammate into a
sleeping bag, tied him to the end of a rope, and slowly began making
their way down.

The rescue operation was a risky one, putting every member of
the team in harm's way, but they all knew that leaving Gilkey behind
was tantamount to a death sentence. So, the entire team took turns
in helping with the descent, each keenly aware of the risks they faced
on K2, a peak that was so dangerous it had earned the nickname
"the Savage Mountain."

At one point, the group reached a section of the climb that an-
gled away very steeply before ending at a cliff face that featured a
drop-off of several thousand feet. They all knew this was going to be

a tricky section to cross and that one wrong move could cost them their lives. Roped together in pairs, the men slowly and cautiously proceeded, bringing Gilkey—still wrapped in his sleeping bag—along as best they could.

As the squad was getting ready to slowly pull their sick comrade across this tricky section, Bell suddenly lost his footing and tumbled down the side of the mountain, pulling Streather along with him. As the two men slid headlong toward the edge of the cliff, their ropes tangled with those being used by Houston and Bates, yanking them off their feet, too. To make matters worse, as they slid towards the edge they barreled headlong into Molenaar who was roped up with Gilkey. In a manner of seconds the entire group went careening toward disaster.

While all of this was happening, Schoening was on belay for Molennar and Gilkey. That meant he was responsible for feeding them the rope they needed to proceed across the incredibly steep section of the climb while also preventing them from falling to their deaths should they slip along the way. When he saw the accident occur right before his eyes, he quickly turned and grabbed onto his ice axe, which had been wedged into the ground nearby. Holding on with all of his strength, and through his own sheer force of will, he managed to arrest the fall of every one of his teammates, preventing the entire squad from plummeting over the edge.

Shaken and exhausted, each of the men gathered himself, climbed to his feet, and began recovering all of the gear that had been discarded during the fall. Such a close call had frayed their nerves, so they decided to trek to a safe spot nearby to set up an emergency camp for the night. Before doing so, they anchored Gilkey to the side of the mountain, telling him they would return once things were secure. But after they had established their campsite, they came back to find that their teammate had vanished without a trace. Apparently while they were away an avalanche hit the slope and swept him over the cliff, never to be seen again.

The rest of the team made it off the mountain safely however and went on to lead long and full lives. But if it wasn't for the quick thinking of Pete Schoening things could have been very different and the first American expedition to K2 would be remembered as a major catastrophe. Instead, Schoening's actions have gone down in mountaineering lore and the incident is now known simply as "The Belay." Generations of climbers that have followed these men still talk about it in reverent terms, marveling at his quick thinking and strength of will, which ended up saving the lives of the entire team.

Most of us won't ever find ourselves clinging to the side of a mountain in an effort to prevent our friends from falling off a cliff face. Still, there are probably going to be times when we'll need to be "on belay" for those around us in some fashion or another. Plans change, things go awry, and unexpected disasters can create havoc. Quick thinking, a strong mindset, and plenty of determination can see us through those experiences and allow us to go on to not only accomplish our goals but allow others to do the same.

My training with the Navy SEALs has provided me with plenty of skills. I've learned how to effectively use small arms and explosives, how to safely parachute from an aircraft, and how to escape from the clutches of enemy forces. I've learned how to treat a wide variety of injuries and can navigate effectively using only a map and compass. I've learned the value of functioning as part of a highly trained team, with each member serving a very specific and important purpose.

But the most important lessons I gained through my training and years of service with the SEALs had nothing to do with those tangible skills. Instead it was about forging a tough, never-quit attitude that could see me through anything that came my way in both my personal and professional life. The discipline I learned in the military allowed me to push myself to greater heights as an athlete and in business too, providing tools that are essential to success.

Once a trainee finishes BUD/S and SEAL Qualification Training, he officially becomes a Navy SEAL, earning the SEAL Trident. This badge is worn with pride by everyone who earns the right to pin it on their uniform. But every SEAL knows that earning your Trident isn't the end of the journey; in fact, it's just the beginning. We constantly operated under the premise that we have to earn our Trident each and every day, proving that we are the best trained, the most physically fit, the toughest, and most feared and effective warriors on the planet. To do that, we worked incredibly hard, and when duty called, we were more than prepared to meet the challenges that were put before us. Complacent is not a word you would ever use to describe a Navy SEAL.

But that attitude can easily be applied to non-SEALs as well. Whatever it is you want to achieve in life, you won't get there by standing still and waiting for success to fall into your lap. Instead, you have to go out and pursue your goals and passions with a purpose. Train for that marathon, climb that mountain, and learn whatever it is you need to learn to reach your objectives. In order to be a success, sometimes you need to shake things up and make things happen. Operating under the assumption that you need to prove yourself each and every day can ultimately help to keep you motivated and focused. And you always need to stay focused on the mission, whatever that might be.

I like to say that it is when things are darkest that we must focus in order to see the light. I truly believe that when things are at their worst, if we just stop to take a little time to think about our objectives and look for a proper solution, one will usually appear. But if you panic or overreact, you may miss an obvious answer to the problem. Stay focused and the light will be revealed.

Not giving 100 percent as a SEAL was never an option and should never be an option in any reputable profession. If you care about what you do and want to be a success, you have to give it your all. If you don't, you're not only selling yourself short but you're letting your teammates down too. Those are things that simply aren't acceptable for a SEAL. Why would they be in other walks of life either?

Expect more from yourself and your team, stay flexible and focused, pursue your goals, and continue to learn new things. If you adhere to those standards you'll be well on your way to earning your own Trident each and every day, no matter what it is you do in life.

MARCUS LUTTRELL
Navy Seal

Most Navy SEALs go about their jobs without anyone ever knowing what it is they do. That's because their missions are usually highly classified with the exact details kept tightly under wraps. But occasionally we get a look behind the curtain to catch a glimpse of what these extraordinary men are capable of accomplishing. Such was the case of Marcus Luttrell, a man whose story you probably already know even if you don't recognize his name.

Born and raised in Houston, Texas, Marcus joined the Navy in 1999 and after completing basic training, went on to become a corpsman. From there, he set his sights on joining the SEALs, completing his BUD/S training in 2000 and earning his Navy Special Warfare Insignia —his SEAL Trident— the following year. After that, he continued his training in a variety of areas before being assigned to SEAL Team Five and getting deployed to Iraq in 2003. His job was to assist in the hunt for WMDs and combat the rising Iraqi insurgency.

In 2005, Marcus was transferred to SEAL Team Ten and sent to Afghanistan as part of SEAL Delivery Vehicle Team One. Not long after he arrived in-country, he and three other SEALs were assigned to take part in a mission dubbed Operation Red Wings. Their objective was to disrupt resistance in the Kunar Province where a local Taliban warlord named Ahmad Shah was causing problems for the regional government.

Marcus and the other three SEALs formed a reconnaissance and surveillance team that would be inserted into a remote region of the Kunar Province. The plan was to drop them off about a mile or so from a village that they were tasked with observing, allowing the four men to set up camp in the hills and watch over the area closely. Their orders were to collect as much intel on the movement of local militia forces as possible without engaging the enemy unless there were no other options.

The SEALs fast-roped out of a helicopter and soon made their way to a favorable vantage point overlooking their target area. They settled in for the mission and tried to remain as stealthy as possible, all the while recording the movements of the Taliban forces, along with the comings and goings of its leadership.

Everything was going according to plan until local goat herders stumbled across the team's covert position while moving their flock into the hills for grazing. The SEALs quickly grabbed the Afghani men but upon realizing that they were unarmed civilians, they let them go. The rules of engagement didn't allow them to do much of anything else so all they could do was release the farmers and hope that real trouble would likely follow.

Knowing that the goat herders were more than likely going to alert the local militia to the SEAL team's presence, the four men dropped back and took cover higher up in the hills. They barely had enough time to find a secure location when a large group of heavily armed men were spotted coming up the hill to find them. The militia members were carrying AK-47 assault rifles and rocket-propelled grenades and didn't look like they were in any mood to negotiate.

Assaulting the SEALs' position from three sides, the team was quickly penned in and found themselves in deep trouble. Gunfire game from just about everywhere and RPGs exploded all around them too. The four Americans fought back desperately, killing a number of the Taliban. But as the fight raged on for what seemed like hours the SEALs found themselves exhausted, wounded, and desperate.

On more than one occasion, the SEALs tried to use both their radios and a satellite phone to alert command to their situation. Pinned down by enemy fire, the team was in need of back-up, but none of the communications devices were functioning properly. They did manage to get a brief message through indicating that they were being attacked but no other details could be shared. In the heat of the battle, there was little time to troubleshoot their malfunctioning equipment.

With no assistance coming and the Taliban forces closing in, the SEALs continued to take heavy fire. Eventually, they were completely overrun and three of the men were killed by the members of the militia. One of the Afghani militants tossed a grenade at Luttrell who was blown into a ravine by the blast, knocking him unconscious and severely wounding him.

When he came to, Luttrell was in agony. He had been shot several times, shrapnel was embedded in his legs, and had severe facial damage, including a broken nose. Later he would learn that he had also broken his back, tore up his shoulder, and suffered damage to his knees as well. Injured, disoriented, and all alone, he crawled into a crevasse and stayed there for a long time, hoping beyond hope that the Taliban forces would just pass him by.

After nightfall, Luttrell pulled himself out of his hiding spot and went on the move. Every part of his body was in pain but he knew that he couldn't stay hidden in the crevasse forever. He needed to find safety and he had no food, water, or supplies to help keep him alive. The Taliban may or may not find him and kill him, but if he stayed where he was, he was as good as dead.

Despite his injuries he was able to walk, stumble, and sometimes crawl in an effort to get away from his attackers. Eventually he found a waterfall and was able to not only take in some much-needed water, but clean his wounds too. He was exhausted, hungry, and in shock, but at least he was alive. As long he still took a breath, there was hope.

It wasn't long after that that several villagers found the SEAL near the waterfall. They quickly told him that they weren't Taliban and that they wanted to help. They led Luttrell to their village and one of the locals took Luttrell into his home. The entire village protected the American from the men that were searching for him, denying they knew his whereabouts. If the militants had discovered where he was, they would have more than likely killed everyone, but the Afghani people did what they could to help, even at great risk to themselves.

Eventually one of the villagers ran to a nearby American military base carrying a note written by Luttrell himself. The note informed the base of Luttrell's location and his current situation. It said he was alive but needed medical attention. This caused the Army to dispatch a team of Rangers to retrieve the SEAL, pulling him out just as the Taliban were closing in on his position.

It would take months for Luttrell to recover from his injuries but when he did, he went back on active duty, rejoining SEAL Team Five in Iraq. He would continue to serve for another year before suffering further injuries, forcing him to retire from the Navy altogether. Before he returned home however, he was awarded the Purple Heart and Navy Cross for his efforts in Operation Red Wings.

Once home, Luttrell would write a book, *Lone Survivor* (2007), which shared his story with the world. The book was later turned into a major motion picture starring Mark Wahlberg, bringing Marcus's ordeal to the big screen as well. He would also launch the Lone Survivor Foundation, a nonprofit dedicated to helping US servicemen and women transition back to civilian life after their time in the military.

In surviving his ordeal in the Kunar Province, Marcus Luttrell demonstrated his own physical and mental toughness. He suffered severe injuries at the hands of his attackers and yet still found the courage and strength to continue on. Despite pain, dehydration, and hunger, he was able to propel himself forward until he could find help. And when he was rescued, brought home, and fully recovered, he immediately resumed his duties as a SEAL. At his retirement, he still honored his commitment to fellow military personnel by founding an organization dedicated to helping them after they return home.

Marcus Luttrell is proof personified that tough, resourceful, and resilient people can accomplish big things if they set their mind to it. It would have been very easy for him to give up while trapped in the mountains in Afghanistan. No one would have blamed him if he had retired from the military after he recovered from his injuries. He could have easily gone home and lived a quiet civilian life. But that isn't the kind of man that he is and quitting wasn't ever a consideration.

Remember that the next time you're facing what seems like overwhelming odds and feeling like you might want to throw in the towel. Your decision to do so may not be a matter of life and death, but it could still have far-reaching consequences that could stick with you or your loved ones for the rest of your life.

Chapter 7

TALES FROM THE BATTLEFIELD

"It is not the mountain that we conquer, but ourselves."
—Sir Edmund Hillary

By its purest definition, a battlefield is often described as a place of conflict, contention, or active opposition. Using that as a basis for our discussion, it is probably safe to say that we have all been on a battlefield of one kind or another at some point in our lives. Whether it be on the athletic field, in a boardroom, high on a remote mountain, or as part of an actual military operation, most of us have had to deal with hostile forces in one form or another. How we reacted to those challenges is probably what ultimately defined our success or failure.

As a Navy SEAL, endurance athlete, and business owner, I have faced "active opposition" in many forms. Whether it was armed gunmen intent on taking my life or other athletes who simply wanted nothing more than to leave me in their wake, there has always been someone actively trying to prevent me from reaching my objectives. Chances are, you've faced similar situations on a regular basis throughout your life too, even if you didn't always recognize the fact that you were facing down "enemy forces."

If you ask someone who is trained in tactics, they're likely to tell you that battles are won by first identifying your objectives and then creating a proper plan to help you achieve those goals. Finding a way to execute that plan, even when things go wrong, is crucial to the success of the mission as well, which is why considering possible contingencies is a smart approach in combat, athletic competitions, business, and life in general.

Most battles are won and lost on the training ground long before they actually begin. That's where we build the necessary skills, conditioning, and mindset that allow us to execute the plan with precision. That way, when we're called upon to perform, we've already gone through the motions many times over and know our roles backwards and forwards. In other words, those who are better prepared will ultimately be more successful. In the SEAL Teams, we live by the motto that "the more sweat and tears you put into training, the less bloodshed in time of war."

In the case of a marathon runner, the battlefield is the race course, the battle is the race itself, and the other competitors are the opposing forces. If the runner shows up to the event well prepared—having put in the required quality training miles—he or she is more likely to find themselves contending for a respectable finish and possibly even a "PR," or personal record. But, if they didn't train as hard as they should have or took the competition too lightly, they could easily come away with a disappointing and even quite a painful finish.

The same holds true for the business professionals squaring off against the competition in the boardroom. In this case, the battlefield is the boardroom itself and the battle is the negotiations and compromises that come along with hammering out a deal. Anyone who wades into that arena needs to do their homework ahead of time and should study the "enemy" in the same way that athletes assess their rivals. Armed with that knowledge, they'll be far better prepared to achieve their objectives, whatever those happen to be.

Sometimes the battlefields that we find ourselves on are of our own creation. When we set goals for ourselves that are more focused on personal improvement, we aren't competing against anyone else but ourselves. Examples of this include embarking on a weight loss program or an exercise regimen designed to help us get into better shape. In those instances, the hostile forces that are working against us are our own insecurities and doubts, which are a common foe that we all face at some point.

At other times, we find ourselves on battlefields in which the world around us is our adversary, which is typically the case when climbing a mountain for example. We aren't competing against any other mountaineers in our attempt to reach the summit, but Mother Nature herself could provide plenty of obstacles in the form of bad weather, poor visibility, and unstable conditions. In order to achieve our goals in those situations we must still overcome our own self-doubt while battling the environment around us too.

The upside of finding yourself on a personal battlefield is that it tends to bring out the best in us. When facing adversity and challenge, the human spirit can come alive, allowing us to accomplish amazing things. It is at those times that you truly push beyond your own boundaries and start to catch a glimpse of everything that you are capable of.

This is something that triathlete Julie Moss is quite familiar with. When she embarked on her first Ironman race at the World Championship in Kona, Hawaii back in 1982, she had no idea that she would not only put in an incredibly inspiring performance but would also take the central role in the most famous finish the event has ever seen.

In 1982, Julie was in her senior year of college at Cal Poly, San Luis Obispo where she was studying physical education. When it came time to write her senior thesis, she was unsure of what her topic should be; but one Saturday she turned on the television to find ABC's "Wide World of Sports" broadcasting the Ironman competition in Kona. Completely enthralled with what she was watching unfold on the screen, she soon came to realize that she had discovered the topic she had been looking for. Right then she decided that she wanted to write about the psychological and physical training aspects of long-distance endurance sports, exploring what went on in the minds and bodies of these extreme athletes as they trained for a race. In order to do that, she first had to go through that experience herself.

The idea of competing in such an event was completely foreign to the twenty-three-year-old Moss. While she was studying PE in college, she wasn't exactly the quintessential jock herself, spending most of her time focusing solely on surfing. To prepare for Kona, however, she took part in a half-Ironman race and ran a couple of full marathons to test her physical endurance. Those races gave her the confidence she needed to know that she could cover the distances required to at least finish the event, even if she ended up far back in the pack.

But when it came time to compete in Hawaii, that wasn't what happened at all; in fact far from it.

After completing the swim and the bike ride Julie found herself in third place heading into the running stage. She quickly passed through the transition area, headed out onto the road, and soon blew by the only two women in front of her. Despite not training particularly hard, she was leading the race and feeling very strong as she headed for home.

Kona is a tough place to win however, particularly for someone who hasn't been there before. Julie found this out the hard way when twenty-five miles into the marathon her legs began to give out. Exhausted, dehydrated, and at the end of her rope, she tried to push onward, willing herself towards the finish line. She ended up collapsing several times in the final mile as every fiber of her being screamed for her to just stop and end the pain.

With about fifteen feet to go to the finish line, Julie collapsed for the final time. As she lay on the ground writhing in agony, another racer by the name of Kathleen McCartney slipped past her in the darkness to claim victory. She had come up just short of winning the race, despite her lack of experience and training.

For her part, McCartney was completely unaware that she had passed Julie on her way to the finish line. She had no idea she had won the race until Ironman officials told her she had finished first. It had never dawned on her that she had managed to somehow catch her rival, and shocked at this revelation, she turned to look over her shoulder to witness something that would go down as one of the seminal events in triathlon history.

No longer able to muster the strength to even climb back onto her feet, Julie began to crawl towards the finish line on her hands and knees. Even though she was in complete agony, she willed herself to keep moving forward. Her body may have quit on her, but her mind was still as determined as ever. Despite bonking hard and even defecating on herself, she still had to cross the finish line and complete the race.

With thousands of spectators on hand to watch the event live, and millions more glued to their televisions at home, Julie Moss managed to cover the remaining few yards and reach the finish line. She would end up claiming second place, just twenty-nine seconds behind McCartney. That remains the closest margin of victory at the Ironman World Championship for both men and women to this day.

Video of Julie's performance went viral in an age long before the Internet had coined the term. Every newscast across the country—not to mention hundreds of other outlets around the world—shared the footage. It was a tremendous display of courage and determination that brought the Ironman competition the attention it needed to blow up into the next big thing in the world of endurance sports. But more than that, Julie Moss would inspire countless others to pursue their goals and never give up, even when things looked their most dire. After all, if this tiny young college student from California could will her way to the finish line, why couldn't the rest of us do it too?

There are a number of lessons that we can take away from Julie's story, not the least of which is that it is extremely hard to beat a person who never gives up. It doesn't matter if you bring that attitude with you out onto the playing field, into the gym, your business, or just daily life; if you refuse to give up, stay focused on reaching your goals, and continually find ways to overcome adversity, chances are good things will happen. It is then that you'll begin to realize that strength doesn't come from what you can do, but instead comes from overcoming the things that you once thought you couldn't do.

Such was the case with my friend Angelika Castaneda, who remains to this day one of the toughest, most determined people I have ever met—including many of the Navy SEALs that I've worked with over the years. Born in Austria, Angelika is one of those extremely talented people who have worn many different hats over the years. At various times throughout her life she has been an ultrarunner, a top tier ultra-triathlete, and an adventure racer. She's also been an entrepreneur, business woman, and fashion model. She even served as Farah Fawcett's stunt double for a time.

In 1997 I put together a team to take part in the Raid Gauloises held in Lesotho, South Africa. "The Raid" is often referred to as "the toughest endurance event in the world" and is legendary for its difficulty. While Ironman races are typically measured in hours, adventure races are often measured in days and sometimes weeks; and while most marathons and triathlons are held on paved roads, these events typically take place in some of the most remote corners of the planet with courses passing through mountains, deserts, and jungles.

Adventure racers usually compete on coed teams of three to five, and typically are required to navigate a course on foot, mountain bike, canoe, raft, and/or kayak. It is also not unusual for races to add climbing, rappelling, orienteering, swimming, or a host of other demanding human-powered activities into the mix as well.

To make things even more difficult, adventures races are nonstop affairs, which means that once the starting gun goes off, the clock doesn't stop ticking until a team reaches the finish line. That typically takes days to accomplish, so it is up to the athletes themselves to decide exactly when they want to stop for recovery, get some sleep, and eat some food. Because of this, the sport is extremely demanding on the body, causing participants to become ill, get disoriented, bonk, pass out, and even hallucinate from sleep deprivation. To say that I was very much drawn to this challenge, would be an understatement. I allowed the sport to take over my life for a time and I enjoyed every second of the journey.

The team dynamics of an adventure race have always been one of its most intriguing elements of the sport. The entire team must stay within fifty or one hundred yards of each other at all times, and since they're pushing each other to the absolute limit throughout the race, it is crucial that everyone gets along well. A team of

Don on his bike training for a winter time trial.

Don on a cross-the-continent paddle in Chile. He competes regularly in kayak competitions and has paddled from Key Largo to Key West, across the country of Chile and most recently paddled a 750-mile paddle in northern Canada.

Don in his kayak preparing for a surf-sky competition.

Ang Dorje Sherpa with Don during their 2016 Everest climb. Ang Dorje is one of the world's best known and most experienced Sherpas on Everest. He has summited the mountain nineteen times and is best known for his heroic efforts during the 1996 disaster when a freak storm led to the deaths of eight climbers.

Ang Dorje Sherpa observing a Tibetan monk blessing Don during his trek to Everest Base Camp.

Rob O'Neill, the Navy SEAL who killed Osama bin Laden during the raid on the Abbottabad, Pakistan, compound on May 2, 2011, enjoying a drink with Don.

Ed Viesturs and Don at Everest base camp. Ed Viesturs is the only American to have climbed all fourteen of the world's 8,000 meter peaks, and the fifth person to do so without using supplemental oxygen. Ed has summited peaks of over eight thousand meters on twenty-one occasions, including Everest seven times. He also took part in the 1998 IMAX filming of *Everest* shortly after the 1996 climbing disaster, which became the highest-grossing documentary up to that time.

Don as he prepares to summit Denali in 2007. Denali, the highest peak in North America (20,310 feet), is considered to be one of the coldest mountains in the world.

Don with a strong team of climbers on Everest 2016.

Don finishing what is considered the toughest hill climb in the world, the summit of New Hampshire's Mount Washington—the highest peak in New England with an average gradient of 12 percent and reaching gradients of up to 22 percent.

Don on Mount Everest.

Don competing in the Horny Toad Invitational Triathlon in 1984.

Marcus Luttrell and his SEAL team. Luttrell is third from right.

Eddy Merckx is a Belgian former professional road and track cyclist. He is widely recognized as the most successful rider in the history of the sport.

Jane Goodall is a scientist who fundamentally changed the way we view primates—and ourselves—through her groundbreaking research in Africa. *(Photo courtesy of Adrián Zoltán/Flickr)*

Edmund Hillary was the first man to reach the summit of Mount Everest in 1953.

Winston Churchill.

Steve Jobs and Bill Gates. *Courtesy of Magnus Manske.*

Reinhold Messner is an Italian mountaineer, adventurer, and explorer who made the first solo ascent of Mount Everest, the first ascent of Everest without supplemental oxygen, along with Peter Habeler, and was the first climber to ascend all fourteen peaks over 8,000 meters (26,000 feet) above sea level. He was also the first person to cross Antarctica and Greenland and he crossed the Gobi Desert alone. Messner also published more than eighty books about his experiences as a climber and explorer.

Roald Amundsen was a Norwegian explorer of the polar regions. He was the leader of the Antarctic expedition of 1910–1912, which was the first to reach the South Pole. He was also the first expedition leader for the air expedition to the North Pole, making him the first person to reach both poles. He is also known as having the first expedition to traverse the Northwest Passage in the Arctic.

When Don was Lead Climber of SEAL Team Six, he and his team had to remain proficient at rock climbing, mountaineering, climbing ships and oil rigs, and scaling buildings.

outstanding athletes who dislike each other will crumble under the demands of a long, arduous race, while those who work well with one another, and support each other throughout, will often come through the ordeal okay.

When I recruited Angelika to the team I already knew that she was an extremely accomplished endurance athlete. But, I had also seen her hit the wall while competing in another ultra-distance adventure race. She had bonked so hard that she was actually crawling on her hands and knees, and eventually even passed out. Prior to the start of the race in South Africa, the two of us were having lunch with a reporter when I expressed some concerns about her eating enough food prior to the start of the event. After all, she would need all of the calories she could get to finish the five-hundred-mile, ten-day competition. What she told me next is something that has stuck with me for years and provides all of the insight you could ever need into her character.

After hearing me voice my reservations, Angelika looked me directly in the eye, and in her thick Austrian accent said, "Don, I will not die on you. I might feel like I'm going to die, but I will not die. My body will eat from itself."

That was a powerful statement and it let me know right then and there that she was not only prepared for the race but was also just as determined as I was—maybe even more so—to reach the finish line as quickly as humanly possible. We went on to run, ride, climb, and paddle our way across a spectacular course in South Africa and Lesotho and ended up having a fantastic season in general, finishing in the top ten of all adventure racing teams in the world that year.

Angelika played a major role in that accomplishment, proving time and again that she was as tough as any of the men on the team. In fact, there were times when I thought she was actually the toughest person on our team. Case in point: during an adventure race the human body takes a great deal of punishment. We'd often use duct tape, super glue, and other common household items to cover blisters, cuts, and minor wounds. But, taking care of your feet is always a challenge and it is not unheard of for racers to lose some of their toenails in the middle of a race due to the constant stress and rubbing. I would come to discover that this wasn't an issue for Angelika, however.

During our race in South Africa I was in the middle of removing my seventh toenail when she walked over to see what I was up to. She looked at me with a bit of distain in her eye before chiding me once again in that Austrian accent. "Don," she said lightly. "If you're serious about these races you'll have your toenails removed before the race. Have them pulled out and have the skin sewn together so they don't grow back."

The whole exchange was so matter of fact that it took me a second to comprehend what she had just told me. Of course, Angelika had already undergone the procedure and didn't have to worry about her toenails at all. I knew right then that she wasn't just a fierce competitor but also was willing to do whatever it took to reach her goals. My respect for her only increased as a result.

As a Navy SEAL, I've had to spend a great deal of time in and around water, both while training and on missions. Considering the nature of the operations that SEALs are tasked with, it is vitally important that we are comfortable and calm, even while spending hours at a time in oceans, lakes, and rivers. Still, it is hard to imagine undertaking some of the challenges that Diana Nyad has faced throughout her long career as an endurance swimmer.

Nyad first came to the attention of the American public back in 1975, when she swam around the entire island of Manhattan in New York City, which took a little under eight hours to complete. A few years later, she made headlines once again by swimming from Bimini Beach in the Bahamas to Juno Beach, Florida, covering 102 miles in 27.5 hours, going nonstop the entire way. During that challenge she set a record for the longest distance open water swim without a wetsuit or shark cage, a record that still stands to this day.

Most of us remember Nyad for her successful swim from Cuba to Florida in 2013 when she was sixty-four years old. It took her fifty-three hours to travel from Havana to Key West, covering 110 miles along the way. A support ship tracked her every move to ensure she remained safe at all times, and at the end of the very long days in the water, she would rest aboard that vessel before resuming the open-water crossing the following morning. It was an intense, grueling journey that served as the perfect example of what we can accomplish if we dedicate ourselves wholeheartedly to a project.

What most people don't remember about Nyad's story however is that this wasn't her first attempt at swimming from Cuba to the US. In fact, it took her five tries before she finally found success, which came more than thirty-five years after she initially set a goal of swimming across the Strait of Florida along the edge of the Gulf of Mexico.

Diana's first attempt at the swim took place in 1978, when she was just twenty-eight years old and in the prime of her athletic career. Strong winds and big waves pushed her off course however and forced her to pull the plug on that aquatic journey some seventy-six miles in. Exhausted and with her hopes dashed, she returned home and eventually retired from competitive swimming altogether, leaving an impressive legacy of endurance feats in her wake.

But the idea of completing that swim never strayed far from her mind, and she came to see it as a significant goal that she had left undone. As the years passed, she began thinking about it more and more, and in 2010 she decided to start training for another attempt. It had been more than thirty years since she last tried swimming such a long distance in open water, and yet she still felt like she had unfinished business in the choppy waters between the US and Cuba.

In 2011, Nyad made two attempts at the long-distance swim, but strong winds and ocean currents put a halt to both tries. Worse yet, painful jelly fish stings made it impossible to continue, leaving her body sore beyond words. Still, she wasn't ready to give up, and in 2012 she managed to swim further than on any of the previous attempts, and yet was still forced to admit defeat due to two large storms that were bearing down on her location.

By 2013, she knew she was physically and mentally fit enough to make the crossing, but she still needed the weather conditions to be just right. For her fifth and final attempt she wore a specially-designed wetsuit that would protect her from jellyfish as well, which ultimately played a crucial role in her success, allowing her to complete the long-distance swim at long last.

There is so much that we can learn from Nyad's story that it is difficult to know just where to begin. The fact that she had set a goal, and was able to see it through, even though it took thirty-five years to do so, is a testament to her strength and determination. Over the course of those three-and-a-half decades Diana didn't get stronger and faster, but she was able to adopt a tougher mindset. That proved to be an invaluable weapon and a key to her success, which when paired with her never-give-up attitude allowed her to keep moving forward despite countless setbacks.

On the surface, it would be easy to define Diana's battlefield as the open ocean itself. After all, it was the strong currents, big waves, and jellyfish that consistently conspired against her to prevent her from achieving her goals. In reality however, she faced some rather big battles within her own mind, where she routinely faced uncertainty and fear. Eventually, she was able to overcome all of the self-doubt and fear of failure, and forge ahead. For her, the idea of giving up on a dream was far harder to take, and not trying was never an option. Remember, regrets from not trying can last a lifetime, and Diana had already waited long enough to realize her goal.

In terms of inspirational athletes, they don't come much more impressive than Kilian Jornet. The Spanish ultra-runner is one of the fastest humans on the planet when it comes to long distance events, particularly those that are fifty or one hundred miles in length. Born and raised in the Pyrenees, he first made a name for himself as a mountain runner and has gone on to dominate numerous ultramarathon events, including some of the toughest races in the world.

In 2010, Jornet launched a personal project he called "Summits of My Life," in which he announced that he would attempt to set speed records on some of the tallest mountains on the planet, culminating with an attempt on Everest itself. Until that point, he was mostly known as an endurance athlete, rather than a mountaineer, but nevertheless he set a goal to achieve the "fastest known time" (FKT) on several famous peaks, including Kilimanjaro, Elbrus, Denali, and Aconcagua—the tallest mountains in Africa, Europe, and North and South America respectively.

Over the course of the next few years, Kilian went on to

systematically knock off each of those peaks, and several others in the Alps as well. Along the way, he set a blistering pace summiting Kilimanjaro in just seven hours and fourteen minutes and Denali in a mind-blowing eleven hours and forty-eight minutes, both of which were speed records at the time. Those mountains typically take the rest of us days to climb, but the Spaniard was doing it in a matter of just a few hours.

Eventually, there was just one mountain left on his "Summits of My Life" bucket list, and in the autumn of 2016, Jornet traveled to the Himalayas to make his attempt on Everest. As usual, he did so with very little fanfare—just a small support team—and the lightest mountaineering gear he could find. Unfortunately, the weather is far more unpredictable in the fall and the conditions were never right for him to truly take a shot at the summit. So, after a few weeks in base camp waiting and watching the skies, he decided to pull the plug and go home.

Undaunted however, the Spanish ultra-athlete returned in the spring of 2017 to give it another try. For a warmup, he first summited Cho Oyu, the sixth highest mountain in the word at 26,906 feet. Then, Jornet moved over to the North Side of Everest in Tibet, which offers just as challenging of an ascent as the South Side in Nepal, but with fewer climbers to get in his way.

For mountaineers, Everest is a formidable battlefield indeed. Not only do alpinists have to deal with high winds, ever-changing weather conditions, and steep slopes, but the thin air makes taking every step feel like a monumental task. At the summit, the atmosphere has roughly 33 percent of the oxygen that is available at sea level, which is why the vast majority of climbers wear oxygen tanks and masks. This provides them with a steady supply of air, but even that equipment can't completely overcome the dramatic change in atmosphere.

A handful of the fittest climbers will forego the use of oxygen altogether however, adding yet another layer of challenge to an ascent of Everest. While several hundred people reach the summit of the mountain in any given year, less than a dozen of those typically do so without wearing an oxygen bottle. Of course, not one to shy away from a challenge, Jornet saw this as the only way to attempt his speed record, so he left the tank and mask behind. He knew full well that the bulky gear would only slow him down.

When a team of climbers launches its summit bid on Everest, it typically takes them about four or five days to reach the top of the mountain. They'll leave base camp and climb up to Camp 1 on the first day, then proceed to Camp 2 on the second day, and so on. Eventually, they'll be in a position to leave Camp 4 for the summit, which they'll try to reach as quickly as they can, then descend back to the campsite for a much-needed rest before dropping all the way back to base camp the following day. This usually comes after several weeks of acclimatization and preparation that helps the body adapt to the thinner air.

But that isn't what Kilian did at all. Instead, he left base camp around 10:00 p.m. on a Saturday and made a single push to the top of the mountain, only stopping long enough to change into warmer gear and take in some food and water along the way. He moved fast and light, calling on all of his years of training as a mountain runner and endurance athlete, to help keep him going throughout the night and all of the following day.

Everything was going very well until Jornet reached an altitude of 25,200 feet. It was about then that he started to experience stomach cramps, vomiting, and diarrhea, which ended up slowing his pace significantly. At that point he started to question whether or not he was going to make it at all and nearly turned back on several occasions. Being sick in the comfort of your own home is bad enough, but being sick on the tallest mountain in the world is a completely different form of agony.

Despite feeling incredibly ill and dealing with all the regular challenges that come along with an Everest expedition, Jornet pressed on, eventually reaching the summit more than a day after he initially set out. It had taken him just twenty-six hours to go from base camp to the highest point on the planet, which in mountaineering terms is the equivalent of running a sub-two hour marathon. In other words, it marked him as ultra-elite.

Jornet spent the next twelve hours descending back to base

camp, where he was greeted by fellow climbers who provided plenty of congratulatory hugs and handshakes. Everyone knew that they had just witnessed one of the most impressive mountain athletes of all time put in a super-human effort. No one else there could even begin to come close to achieving what the Spanish alpinist had just accomplished.

Exhausted, hungry, and still recovering from his stomach ailment, Jornet retreated to his tent where he crawled into a sleeping bag and was soon sound asleep. But in the back of his mind, he knew that he could've done better. If he hadn't been sick he could have gone faster and set an even more impressive pace. Less than a week later, he would do just that.

Just five days after his initial Everest climb, the Spanish trail runner set out for the summit once again, eschewing the use of oxygen for a second time. He had managed to fend off the stomach bug that had slowed him down a few days earlier and recovered remarkably well in a very short period of time. With his strength returned, Jornet sped up the mountain even more quickly, reaching the top in just seventeen hours. That is an incredible pace for anyone to set, let alone a climber who had already summited the mountain just a few days earlier.

To complete his "Summits of My Life" project, Jornet needed to not only be in phenomenal physical condition, but he had to have the right mindset too. Climbing Everest while sick, completely alone, and without oxygen is amongst the most demanding feats imaginable. The fact that he was able to power through, accomplish his goals, and do it in record time, is amazing. Everest may have been Jornet's personal battlefield, but he overcame all of the opposition that the mountain put in front of him and managed to defeat it not once, but twice. In the process, he left an indelible mark on mountaineering history and his place in it.

Of course, the most famous and important battlefield that any Nave SEAL has ever been on is one that I didn't participate in directly, yet still played a role in nonetheless. I'm talking of course about the assault on Osama bin Laden's compound in Abbottabad, Pakistan, which resulted in the death of the most wanted man in

US history. That mission was conducted by members of SEAL Team Six, a group that almost no one ever talked about prior to May 1, 2011. Technically speaking, Team Six didn't even exist, and yet on that day the whole world knew who they were and what they had accomplished.

For nearly ten years the CIA, NSA, FBI, and various other agencies had been on the hunt for bin Laden. When the US invaded Afghanistan following 9/11, the leader of the Al Qaeda terrorist group went into hiding, staying almost completely off the radar for months on end. Bin Laden knew that if he popped his head up even for a moment, the US would take the opportunity to either capture or kill him. So, he built a secret compound in eastern Pakistan, tried to remain off the grid, and settled into a secluded and secretive life that allowed him to maintain rudimentary communication with his followers while still protecting his location and identity at all times.

By late 2010, some members of the US intelligence community came to believe that bin Laden could be hiding in Abbottabad. Their theory was the result of years of surveillance of various couriers that worked with the Al Qaeda leader, as well as a possible tip from someone within Pakistan. Using assets on the ground, the CIA eventually came to the conclusion that there was indeed a very high-level member of the terrorist group holed up in a walled home located at the heart of the Pakistani city. They weren't 100 percent certain it was bin Laden of course, but there was a strong feeling amongst intelligence experts that they had found the man they had been searching for at long last.

Knowing that bin Laden was extremely paranoid and could potentially move at any time, the Joint Special Operations Command (JSOC for short), working in conjunction with the CIA, began planning an operation that would send US troops on a secret mission into Pakistan. Their job would be to take out this Al Qaeda operative, whoever he was, once and for all. The military officials organizing the raid knew they would need fast, efficient, and highly skilled warriors to conduct the mission, so naturally they turned to SEAL Team Six.

During my time with the SEALs, I served with Team Six from

1985 to 1989 and again from 1995 to 1998. At the time, we were the most highly trained combat unit in the world, but rarely had a chance to put our skills to the test in the field. In contrast, the modern version of SEAL Team Six had been honed to a razor-sharp edge on the battlefield in Iraq and Afghanistan, and is outfitted with equipment and technology that we could only dream of back in the '80s and '90s. As a result, they are now leagues ahead of pretty much any other military unit in the world, which made them the perfect group for this mission.

The plan was a daring one right from the start. Because bin Laden was hiding inside Pakistan, intelligence officials knew they would need to walk a tenuous tightrope. In order to conduct the raid, the US commando team would have to cross into Pakistani territory, but if any high-ranking officials within the country got wind of the operation, there was a good chance they would alert the Al Qaeda leader ahead of time, giving him time to escape.

Eventually the decision was made to keep the operation a complete secret, even from the Pakistani government. The plan was to fly in under the cover of darkness from a US base located in Afghanistan. The May 1 date was specifically chosen because it was a moonless night, providing an extra bit of darkness for the SEALs to conduct their business. It was going to be the most difficult and dangerous mission of their lives, and they would take every advantage they could get.

Using two high-tech Black Hawk helicopters that had been designed for stealth and night operations, the team, which consisted of about two-dozen men, was able to reach bin Laden's compound without being detected. The SEALs then fast-roped into the courtyard below and deployed outside the house. But before they could enter the building, one of the helicopters experienced unusual atmospheric conditions that caused it to momentarily lose control, smashing its tail into the wall that surrounded the compound. This caused it to crash land hard onto the ground, rendering the aircraft inoperable.

The SEALs always had contingency plans. "What if a helo goes down?" Or "What if only half the team can make it to the target?"

and so on. The guys on the downed helo were all okay and in this case all made it to the target too. The loss of the helicopter wasn't good, but it also wasn't crucial to the completion of the mission either.

While attempting to breach a door that led into the house, they discovered that it was actually fake, leading to nowhere. That was their first clue that the person hiding inside was a high-value target, most likely bin Laden himself. But even as they located another door and made their way inside, there was still no real confirmation that they were closing in on the most wanted terrorist on the planet.

Once inside the home, the SEALs broke off into groups and slowly started sweeping through the various rooms that made up the interior. Prior to their arrival, CIA operatives on the ground in Abbottabad cut the power to the entire city block, sending the compound into complete darkness. Night vision goggles allowed the SEALs to continue to do their work with efficiency and precision, as they quickly engaged and dispatched with several hostile individuals living on the first floor.

Several members of the team found a staircase leading upstairs and began to make their way to the second floor. At that point, a bearded man stuck his head around the corner in an effort to see who was coming his direction. The lead SEAL immediately recognized him as bin Laden's son, Khalid, from photos that they were shown while prepping for the raid. The man quickly ducked back around the corner out of sight, but thinking very quickly the SEAL called out his name in Arabic. When Khalid bin Laden looked around the corner a second time to see who had called his name, he was dispatched with a single shot to the head.

Proceeding up the stairs, the team found a second staircase leading to the third floor with another, much older, bearded man standing at the top. They instantly recognized him as Osama bin Laden and one of the SEALs took a shot at the Al Qaeda leader as he rushed into another room. Now they knew exactly who they had in their sights and they moved upward to finish the mission.

When the SEALs reached the top floor, two young girls and an adult woman rushed directly at them in an effort to protect bin

Laden. Fearing that they might be rigged with explosive vests, the first SEAL up the staircase jumped at them in an effort to save his teammates who were not far behind. He knocked all three women to the floor and pinned them there, waiting for the explosion to come. Fortunately, none of the women were actually strapped with bombs, but the selfless act of that SEAL is a testament to his exceptional training, quick thinking, and commitment to both the mission and the other men that he served with.

With that threat dealt with, other members of the team pursued bin Laden into the room in which he had fled. Upon entering, they saw him huddling in corner while holding an AK-47 by his side and shaking very badly. This mastermind of world terror was hiding behind one of his wives, using her as a human shield. Loyal to the end, the woman hurled herself at the men who had come for her husband, but one of the SEALs shot her in the leg before she could get too close. Another SEAL then fired on bin Laden himself, putting a bullet into his forehead and another in his chest. As he slumped to the ground, the shooter put a third round into the Al Qaeda leader, bringing an end to a manhunt that had lasted nearly a decade.

With all threats neutralized, bin Laden's corpse was put into a body bag for transport back to base. The team swept through the house once again, this time gathering up every computer, hard drive, thumb drive, and cell phone that they could find. They also stuffed countless papers and dossiers into bags, much of which would prove to hold important information about the inner workings of Al Qaeda. While taking down the head of that organization was the primary goal of the mission, the data that was gathered would prove invaluable moving forward.

In a testament to just how efficient SEAL Team Six is in the field, consider this: The entire raid was expected to take forty minutes to complete, and the team finished up and were boarding a support helicopter that had come in for the extraction in exactly thirty-eight minutes. Everything had gone like clockwork, and they were in and out completely on schedule. That is the kind of precision work that comes from training like you fight and fighting like you train.

There was one last hurdle that the group had to clear before they were home free however. They still had to get out of Pakistani airspace without getting shot down. The stealth Black Hawk and Chinook support helicopters took off into the night, with every passenger onboard collectively holding his breath. The pilots kept the helos close to the ground so as to avoid radar detection, and for the next hour everyone remained on edge. It was about then that a voice came over the intercom announcing "Here's something you never thought you'd be relieved to hear. Welcome to Afghanistan."

The mission has been a tremendous success and was met with relief and celebrations back in the US. On the evening of May 1, 2011, President Obama went on national television to announce that Osama bin Laden had been killed at long last. It was a pivotal moment in the ongoing fight with Al Qaeda and other terrorist organizations, with the Navy SEALs making headlines around the globe. In fact, the raid had been named Operation Neptune Spear; anyone who remembers their mythology knows that Neptune's spear is actually a three-pronged trident—the same symbol that every SEAL wears with pride.

In the weeks and months that followed, more details emerged about Operation Neptune Spear with countless articles and books being written, and films being made about the daring raid. As the media blitz surrounding the death of bin Laden continued, it was revealed that the SEAL who shot and killed the terrorist leader was Senior Chief Petty Officer Robert O'Neill. I was so very proud of the guys at ST-6. As the Advanced Training Officer of the team, I had the opportunity to train many of the men who took part in that mission. I felt a great sense of satisfaction in knowing that I played a small role in helping bring down the leader of Al Qaeda and the mastermind behind the attacks on the US on 9/11.

Later, I would have the chance to talk to Rob and some of the other SEALs in great detail about the mission, and would gain a lot of insight into what it was like for them. To a man, they all told me that they thought that they were going on a one-way trip and that they wouldn't be coming home. They all knew the risks ahead of time and were sure that if they didn't get shot down by Pakistani fighter jets, bin Laden's compound would offer a high level of resistance that would result in many casualties. Getting out safely seemed like an incredible long shot, with a razor-thin margin for error. And yet they all went on the mission anyway because they knew that it was what needed to be done. It was their job, and each and every one of them was ready to give his life in service to their country.

Prior to embarking on the mission, each of the men wrote letters to friends and family saying their goodbyes. Fortunately, none of those letters ever had to be delivered, as every man came home safely with only a few very minor injuries spread out across the entire team. They executed the plan that they were given with so much precision that several of them told me that the training exercises that I and others put them through were never as easy as what they had encountered in bin Laden's compound. One even said that it was so easy, it was "like shooting at paper targets." They went in as prepared as humanly possible and their dedication and professionalism won the day.

When Rob O'Neill's camouflaged shirt which he wore during the raid was put on display at the 9/11 Memorial Museum in New York City, I was deeply honored to be standing by his side. The last thing bin Laden saw, was Rob's shirt and the American flag on the left shoulder. Rob personally asked me to attend that very moving ceremony and I wouldn't have missed it for the world.

The story of the SEALS who conducted the raid to finally get bin Laden is a good reminder that proper training, finely honed skills, and a tough mindset can prepare you for almost any challenge. That is a lesson that we can all apply to the personal battlefields that we find ourselves on throughout out our lives. If you train like you fight, you'll definitely fight like you train, whatever your fight might be.

EDDY MERCKX
Professional Cyclist

Professional cycling has had its fair share of larger-than-life figures throughout its long and storied history. Men like Greg Lemond, Lance Armstrong, Alberto Contator, and Miguel Indurain have cast long shadows over the sport. But none of them can hold a candle to Belgian rider Eddy Merckx, who is widely viewed as the greatest professional cyclist who has ever lived, with an impressive resume filled with credentials that back up that claim.

Born in Belgium in June of 1945, Merckx rode his first bicycle at the age of four and by the time he was eight he was already riding his bike to school every day. Always a talented athlete Merckx took part in a number of different sports throughout his teenage years, including soccer, basketball, and boxing. But his one true love was always cycling and he began competing in amateur races in 1961 at the age of sixteen. He would win his first event later that same year, but it would only be the first of many to come.

As an amateur, Merckx racked up wins at an astounding rate. In 1962 he competed in fifty-five different races, winning twenty-three of them. He had become so focused on cycling that his grades began to suffer to the point that it looked like he wouldn't graduate high school. But once he won the Belgian amateur cycling championship he elected to not return to school anyway, dropping out so he could focus more on his training.

In 1964, Eddy would concentrate on competing at the Summer Olympics, where he finished twelfth in a large field of talented riders. Later that year he'd win the amateur road race at the UCI Road World Championships, one of the biggest annual events in cycling. With that win under his belt, he decided to give up his amateur status and turn pro instead. When he did, he had eighty victories on his resume.

The following year was Merckx's first as a professional and he managed to win one race despite his relatively young age and inexperience. But he learned a lot that season and soon became a force to be reckoned with in the peloton. In 1966 he would win twenty races, including Milan-San Remo, his first career victory in one of cycling's "Monuments" races—the sports oldest and most prestigious events. It would not be his last.

By 1967 he really started to pick up steam, taking the win at Milan-San Remo again, while also earning two stage victories at the Giro d'Italia, the Grand Tour of Italy. But more importantly, late in the year he won his first ever world championships as a pro, earning the right to wear the coveted rainbow jersey throughout the following year.

By the time Merckx entered his fourth pro season, he had established himself as one of the best all-around riders in the world. While some cyclists were great climbers and others amazing sprinters, he could do both equally well. A select few were even talented enough to contend in the Grand Tours—the Giro d'Italia, the Vuelta a España, and the Tour de France. It was quickly becoming clear that the Belgian was one of them.

Throughout the rest of his career, Merckx was so focused on winning that few athletes in any sport can measure up to his level of dominance. He would go on to win eleven Grand Tours in total, (including five wins at the Tour de France), which is a record that no one has come close to equaling. He would also take home the rainbow jersey as the world champ on three separate occasions, while becoming one of just three men in the history of cycling to claim victory at all five of the Monument races. Over the course of his thirteen-year career he would win twenty-eight other one-day classics too, with only the Paris-Tours race escaping his grasp.

In 1972, Merckx would go after one of the toughest and most demanding records in all of cycling: the hour record. This event challenges a single rider to see how far he can ride in just sixty minutes and requires a maximum effort throughout the entire hour on the bike. The Belgian made his assault on the hour record at an outdoor track in Mexico City and managed to break the record, covering an astounding thirty-one miles before the clock ran out.

To get a clear picture of just how dominant Merckx was out on the road, one need only look to the 1969 Tour de France. Everyone knows that the leader in that race wears the famed yellow jersey, but the Tour also hands out the green jersey to the best sprinter, the white jersey to the best young rider under the age of twenty-five, and the polka-dot jersey to the best climber as well. That year, Merckx came into the race angry, and wasn't about to be denied his place in cycling history.

In the first Grand Tour of the year—the Giro—he was disqualified due to a failed drug test, something that Merckx has disputed to this day. There are some indications that he may have been given a tainted water bottle, which led to his positive result. Either way, at the start of the Tour de France, the Belgian felt he had a lot to prove.

Eddy would go on to ride like a man possessed. He would turn back every challenger and throw down the gauntlet in every way imaginable. He contended in sprints, he racked up points on the climbs, and was unwilling to concede an inch to any of his rivals. In the end, he would win the race easily, finishing seventeen minutes in front of the other two riders who shared the podium with him in Paris.

But that isn't why this race was so special. Not only would Merckx win his first of five yellow jerseys, but he'd also take home the green, white, and polka-dot jerseys too. That meant he wasn't just the best overall rider, he was also the best sprinter, climber, and young cyclist too. This is a feat that has never been equaled and likely never will. In the modern era of cycling where riders are highly specialized in one or two disciplines, it is simply impossible to pull off such a performance ever again.

By the time he retired in 1978, Merckx had recorded the most career victories by a cyclist (525), the most victories at the classics (28), and the most victories at any single race by winning Milan-San Remo seven times. He also has the most stage victories at the Tour de France (34), the most stage victories in a single race (8), and the most days wearing the yellow jersey (96).

Because he was such a dominant force in cycling Merckx earned several not-so-flattering nicknames over the years. In Italy he was referred to as *il Mostro* which means "the monster." But his most memorable moniker was "the cannibal" given to him by the young daughter of a teammate upon hearing her father say that Eddy wouldn't let anyone else win. The name stuck and seemed fitting to his fearsome personality when competing in a race.

After he retired, Merckx would start his own bike company, serve as the director of the Belgian national championship team, and race director for several events. He's also played key roles in helping launch the Tour of Qatar and Tour of Oman, while serving as a living legend and ambassador for the sport of cycling.

While Merckx was obviously a gifted rider who was both physically strong and possessed great endurance too, the same could be said about many of his rivals. What set the Belgian apart was his never-quit attitude, his ability to ride with a very large chip on his shoulder, and the mental toughness that saw him through some of his worst days on a bike. Fueled by a competitive fire that few athletes possess, he was able to set himself apart from every other cyclist that came before him or since. He was indeed a monster in the peloton, and going into a race against him, you knew you had to be at your very best.

Merckx was known for his attacking style and his ability to leave everything out on the road in an effort to reach the finish line ahead of his rivals. He rarely rode in a defensive fashion and would push himself to the limit one day only to return to the course the next day to do it all over again. He didn't manage to win every race that he entered, but he won far more than his fair share. Perhaps if we are just as aggressive in the pursuit of our goals, we'll get our fair share of victories too.

Chapter 8

ELIMINATING EXCUSES

"Difficulty is the excuse history never accepts."
—Edward R. Murrow

By now you've no doubt realized that successful people have a number of key traits that allow them to accomplish the things they set their mind to. Not only do they possess a tough mindset, but they are also resilient enough to overcome adversity, know how to identify micro-goals and convert them into macro-goals, and always find a way to keep moving towards their objective. They are adaptable, constantly learning new things, and they are usually driven by an inner fire that pushes them onward, because not trying at all is simply not an option.

What these individuals tend not to do however is make excuses. That's because successful people know that excuses only get in the way of achieving our true objectives. An excuse is an easy way out. It is a way of placing the blame for failure on an external force, without acknowledging your own part in the process. In a way, an excuse is like giving yourself a get out of jail free card when it comes to failure.

Worse yet are the people who make excuses to avoid even starting the process of pursuing their goals. They're the ones who say they don't have enough time in their day or they don't possess the talent and knowledge that they need to actually do the things that they want to do. They tell themselves that they're not in good enough physical condition to run a race, or they don't have the money they need to start a business, so why even try? These types of people look to avoid failure altogether by never taking any kind of risk at all.

In actuality, many people who went on to be wildly successful were in the exact same position at some point, but instead of sitting on the bench and watching the rest of the world go by, they decided to jump into the game. They were willing to make the sacrifices or accept the risks that were necessary because not trying wasn't an acceptable option. They found ways to eliminate the excuses and doubts that were lingering in their head in order to push forward, because the reality is that if you want something bad enough, you'll find a way to get it.

Successful people don't look for excuses not to try; they search for solutions that allow them to start. They make time in the evenings and on weekends, they hone their skills and talents in classes and workshops, and they make their goals a priority, rather than some nebulous dream that they're perpetually wondering about. If there is one thing that feels worse than failure, it is the regret of never trying at all and living with the constant question of "what if?"

Arlene Blum is one person who doesn't have to ask herself that question. She entered the ranks of the predominantly male sport of mountaineering in the early 1960s at a time when female climbers were exceedingly rare. Today, the number of women who join expeditions to the Himalayas is growing, but they remain well in the minority. At the start of Blum's career, it was all but unheard of.

Nevertheless, Blum persisted in pursuing her mountaineering ambitions and by 1970 she was part of the first all-women climbing expedition to Denali (aka Mt. McKinley) in Alaska. That endeavor proved highly successful with all six ladies reaching the summit on a mountain that is known for being technically difficult and prone to some of the most horrendous weather on the planet.

Following her success on Denali, Blum went on to summit a variety of other peaks around the world, while building a reputation for being tough and resilient in the mountains. This helped to earn her a spot on the second American expedition to Everest which took place in 1976. Just a year earlier a Japanese climber named Junko Tabei had become the first woman to summit the mountain. Her historic feat came twenty-two years after the first ascent by Edmund Hillary and Tenzing Norgay. Blum was hoping to join the ranks of female Everest summiteers too, but unfortunately, she wasn't selected for the summit team and never climbed higher than 24,500 feet.

Two years later she would return to the Himalayas, but this time in a completely different role, with a different team, and on a very different mountain. In 1978 Blum organized the first all-female expedition to Annapurna, a 26,200-foot peak that is considered by many to be the most difficult and dangerous on the planet. That endeavor proved to be a successful one, putting two of the women, and two Sherpa guides, on the summit, marking the first time that an American—male or female—stood on top of that mountain.

But just getting to Annapurna in the first place was a major obstacle to overcome. During the 1970s there was still a prevailing feeling in mountaineering circles—and society in general—that women weren't as strong, skilled, or as tough as men. This made fundraising for the expedition a real challenge, as few companies were willing to support a team of ladies who wanted to climb an 8,000-meter peak in the Himalayas. At that point, only eight men had ever successfully summited Annapurna while nine others had perished during the attempt.

Without funds, Blum knew that her all-women mountaineering team would see their Himalayan dreams dashed before they would ever begin. Back then—as now—an expedition to the Himalaya costs tens of thousands of dollars, and without corporate sponsorship the ladies would never be able to afford to pay for the trip on their own. Blum knew that she had to come up with a solution, and quickly.

Eventually she decided to sell t-shirts as a fundraiser for the expedition. The team had two different designs that they offered customers, the first of which simply read "Annapurna," which turned out to be a modest seller at best. But the other shirt featured a bold typeface that simply read "A woman's place is on top." It didn't matter that the design included the silhouette of a mountain in the background, as the double entendre alone was enough to sell pretty much every shirt the team could print.

In the end, Blum and the other ladies managed to sell more than 15,000 of those t-shirts, raising over $80,000 in the process. That humble shirt would not only become an iconic piece of mountaineering history, but a rallying cry for female empowerment everywhere. It also paved the way for Arlene Blum and her squad to make a little history of their own on Annapurna.

Faced with obstacles at every turn, questioned by doubters both in and out of the mountaineering community, and lacking the necessary funds to get her expedition off the ground, Blum could have easily called it quits. No one would have blamed her if she had decided to pull the plug due to a lack of corporate sponsorship or having to overcome the logistical challenges of putting a women's only expedition together. But Blum wasn't looking for an excuse to quit, she was looking for ways to make the expedition happen. She had to get creative and be willing to risk a little money upfront when printing the t-shirts, but ultimately that led to a historic expedition that continues to inspire female climbers to this day.

The whole process of creating smaller goals to achieve bigger ones is specifically designed to help eliminate excuses. Achieving any major goal always seems extremely daunting when you're first starting out, but by thinking about the steps you need to get there, and breaking those steps down into smaller, more digestible parts, things become much more manageable.

When a runner sets a goal of completing a marathon, the idea of running 26.2 miles always sounds like an incredibly difficult task, particularly if they've never run that far before. But by creating a training plan that starts small and slowly works its way up to the longer distance, the excuses for not chasing that goal begin to evaporate. Sure, when you get started, running more than twenty-six miles seems impossible. But running just one or two miles doesn't seem so bad.

Over time, the distances increase, but due to your training and improved physical conditioning, the miles become less and less of an issue. Before long, you're ready to tackle a challenge that once seemed way out of reach, in part because you used micro-goals to slowly work your way toward your macro-goals.

No goal worth achieving is ever easy, and almost everyone faces some degree of adversity along the way. When things get tough, it is natural to want to stop or even give up on your dream altogether. That is when we are most likely to start looking for excuses. We tell ourselves that things are just too hard or that we're not talented, smart, or physically fit enough to achieve the things we want to do. Self-doubt begins to creep in and we start to question all of the training and hard work that we've done up until that point. It can be a very demoralizing situation.

But instead of looking for reasons to give up, embrace the challenge instead. Take some time to reassess your micro-goals, examine your plan of action, and push all of the excuses to the side. If you're mentally strong and dedicated to achieving good things, you'll be able to overcome the obstacles that caused you to stumble in the first place. The last thing you need is to create more obstacles for yourself by giving in to the excuses.

If there is anyone who epitomizes this "no excuses" approach to life, it is my friend and fellow SEAL Carlos Moleda. Born and raised in São Paulo, Brazil, he moved to US at the age of eighteen, became a citizen, and eventually joined the Navy. He would go on to be one of just eleven men who graduated from his BUD/S class and would later find himself stationed in Central America and Panama.

In 1989, a number of SEALs were dispatched on a covert mission in Panama to capture General Manuel Noriega's private plane. Both Carlos and I were a part of the operation, with his team heading into a hangar that intel had told us was empty. Instead, it ended up being very well guarded and a firefight ensued. During the battle he took bullets to both his leg and chest, and as a result of those injuries Carlos would end up paralyzed from the sternum down. His career as a SEAL was over at the age of twenty-seven, but he was only just getting started.

Carlos began an intense rehabilitation program designed to help adapt to his disability, which included learning to use a wheelchair to get around. As he progressed through the training, his physical therapist challenged him to compete in a 5K race using a wheelchair, which he would propel along using just his arms and shoulders. The therapist promised Carlos that if he finished the race, she would request that the Veterans Administration get him a specially-designed chair just for racing. He took her up on the challenge and managed to finish the race, although it wasn't easy.

Competing in that event gave Carlos a nice sense of purpose and provided him with a new goal. With his rehab complete, he was ready to focus on something new. He wanted to race, and when his therapist made good on her promise, and the VA delivered a racing chair, he started to do just that.

At first Carlos only competed in shorter events, finishing 5K and 10K races. Over time, he trained harder and got faster, and as his strength and stamina grew, he eventually started entering marathons too. Carlos and I were neighbors which gave us an opportunity to train together regularly. Training with Carlos inspired me a great deal, forcing me to work harder and count my blessings at the same time.

In 1996 Carlos learned that another paralyzed athlete by the name of John Franks was preparing to race the Ironman World Championship at Kona. Intrigued by this possibility and having already achieved his micro-goal of competing in shorter events, he set a new macro-goal. Carlos not only wanted to compete in Hawaii within two years, he wanted to win the race, too.

With that goal in mind, Carlos embarked on what would become quite an adventurous athletic career. Not only would he make good on his goal of winning the Ironman World Championship in just two years, he would repeat that feat on four other occasions. He also won back to back US handcycling championships in 1999 and 2000, and won the 1999 Midnight Sun event, a grueling stage-race that covers 367 miles over nine days.

Not content with those achievements, Carlos has also completed the 3,000-plus-mile Race Across America bike event and in 2016 he even reached the summit of Mt. Kilimanjaro, the tallest mountain in Africa. The fact that he could pedal his handcycle all the way to the top of the 19,341-foot mountain is an impressive and inspiring feat to say the least.

It would have been so easy for Carlos to have simply accepted his fate and decide to not push himself too hard. After all, his injuries gave him the perfect excuse to stop pursuing his goals and live a more sedentary life on the sidelines. But that just isn't the kind of person that he is. When he could no longer be a Navy SEAL, he went looking for other ways to challenge himself both physically and mentally. Unsurprisingly to those of us who know him, Carlos has gone on to be not only a successful athlete, but a businessman, father, and husband too.

The rest of us can take a great deal of inspiration from Carlos's story. If being paralyzed from the sternum down wasn't enough to stop him from competing—and winning—some of the toughest endurance challenges imaginable, why would we allow our relatively insignificant excuses to keep us from doing the things that we want to do too? Think about that the next time you start to question whether or not you can accomplish your own goals. It is hard to say you can't do it when a guy like Carlos Moleda has been making the most of his situation for years.

Another adventure athlete who doesn't have time for excuses is Erik Weihenmayer. That's because he is busy busting stereotypes and proving to the world that a disability of any kind isn't enough to keep you from not only living a normal life, but pursuing really big aspirations along the way too.

When he was just one year old, Weihenmayer was diagnosed with retinoschisis, a disease that attacks the retinas and can often lead to blindness. Throughout his childhood, Erik learned to deal with this condition, which caused his eyesight to degenerate over time, eventually leaving him completely blind at the age of thirteen. Despite that however, he still became an accomplished athlete, serving as the captain of his wrestling team in high school and even competing at the National Junior Freestyle Wrestling Championships.

Even at an early age, Weihenmayer had a passion for the outdoors and was determined to not let his deteriorating eyesight deter him from participating in the activities that he loved. When he was sixteen, Erik tried rock climbing for the very first time and quickly discovered that he had a real knack for the sport. From there, he continued to hike and camp on a regular basis, and eventually he took up high altitude mountaineering as well.

Weihenmayer's first big climb came back in 1995 when he reached the summit of the 20,310-foot Denali in Alaska. His success on that prominent peak only served to fuel his confidence and adventurous ambitions further and he followed that expedition by becoming the first blind person to summit Everest in 2001. The following year he would go on to complete his quest to climb all of the Seven Summits, the highest peaks on each of the seven continents. At the time, only about 150 people had managed to achieve that feat.

For most people, climbing Everest and a half-dozen other prominent peaks around the world would be enough adventure for one lifetime. But in the years that followed, Weihenmayer continued to push boundaries by completing the first blind ascent of the iconic 3,000-foot El Capitan in Yosemite National Park and a frozen waterfall of the same height in Nepal. He has also competed in adventure races including Primal Quest, an adventure race that has been called "The World's Most Challenging Endurance Competition" of which I served as director and CEO. Additionally, Erik has made more than fifty skydives, learned how to ski, and became the first blind solo paraglider as well.

But perhaps his greatest adventure came in 2014, when Erik, along with blind Navy veteran Lonnie Bedwell and a group of their friends, completed a kayaking expedition through the Grand Canyon. The journey covered more than 277 miles along the Colorado River and required three weeks to complete. Along the way, the team faced rapids that were often rated Class 4 or higher on the international scale of river difficulty. That's a level that is plenty challenging for a strong and experienced paddler, whether they can see or not.

Both Weihenmayer and Bedwell paddled their kayaks solo, while teammates offered advice and encouragement over a wireless Bluetooth communications system. This enabled the two men to get a sense of the challenges in front of them, even though they couldn't see them at all. This voice guidance, paired with their own paddling skills and sense of adventure, helped the pair complete the expedition, proving once again that the only limitations that we face are the ones that we put on ourselves.

Time and again Erik has proven that just because he can't see, that doesn't mean that he lacks vision. In a lot of ways, he sees goals and objectives much better than the rest of us. His enthusiasm for life and love of outdoor adventure could have easily been sidelined when he lost his eyesight, but he refused to let that keep him from doing the things that he loves. While smashing stereotypes and preconceived notions along the way, he forces us to reassess what we think is possible.

The blind adventurer lives by a credo that says "what's inside of you is stronger than what's in your way," and he has proven that time and again. The next time you're looking for an excuse to quit on a hard workout, bail on a business plan, or just give up on your goals in general, think about Erik Weihenmayer and the things that he has accomplished simply because he refuses to let his lack of eyesight be a crutch to lean on.

As a Navy SEAL, we rarely had the luxury of being able to offer any kind of excuse either. We were tasked with completing some of the most difficult missions that the US military embarked upon, and our job was to always find a way to get it done. Case in point, one of the most challenging situations that I ever faced in the early years of my career came when I, along with three other SEALs, conducted a highly sensitive demolitions and reconnaissance mission in the Middle East. It was my first real-world operation since joining the team, and the four of us had been handpicked by our commanding officer to conduct the operation.

This was such a highly sensitive and classified mission that we had to go in without any backup, leaving very little room for error. To make matters worse, prior to the start of the mission each of us had eaten frogs, as well as several venomous and nonvenomous snakes, while on a survival training exercise. We would kill the creatures, or at least stun them, by swiftly striking their heads on our boots. Then we'd bite down under their head and peel back the skin to gain access to what little meat that was found there. And while this did provide us with some much-needed nourishment, when coupled with the filthy environment we found ourselves in, we all ended up getting food poisoning. It would soon come back to haunt us.

The mission began when the four of us jumped out of a C-130 aircraft high over the Indian Ocean in the middle of the night. Under the cover of darkness, we parachuted safely into the water below, gathered up our gear—which included a rubber raft called a Zodiac—and began motoring our way into shore. As we drew within 300 meters of the enemy beach, we cut the engine on the boat. From there, one of my teammates and I silently slipped into the water and swam towards the shore to conduct a beach reconnaissance. We had to ensure the beach was clear of enemy personnel and find a secure place to lay up there for three days.

In our mission briefing, we were warned by the intel officers to stay out of the water as much as possible. It seems the locals made it a habit to gut their camels near the shore and throw the organs and intestines into the water not far from the beach that we were approaching. This had the unfortunate consequence of attracting sharks, who would routinely break into a feeding frenzy while devouring the entrails.

When we splashed down into the water, we wasted no time getting into our boat. Needless to say, we were very concerned about those sharks, and my buddy and I did not like the idea of diving back in for a swim to shore. We didn't say a word to each other, but swam as quickly and as quietly as we could, hitting the beach in near record time.

Thankfully we were able to reach the shore without encountering any of the aquatic predators. Once there, we quickly scrambled up onto the sand and began digging two holes, one to bury our non-operational gear and the other for us to hide in for three days while we conducted our reconnaissance mission. We buried the gear with sand and covered our approximately four-foot-by four-foot hole with a piece of desert camouflage netting, which somewhat helped to conceal our position. It provided us the means to see through the netting and gave us a secure place to lay low while we collected information on maritime traffic to and from a nearby shipyard, as well as the aircraft coming and going from a local airstrip.

Extreme heat made it almost unbearable during the day and high winds constantly blew sand and other debris in our direction. Our noses and ears were filled with dust but fortunately our goggles provided some protection for our eyes. Things got even more uncomfortable with the arrival of the high tide, however, as the rising water had a habit of filling up our hole, making it a miserable place to be huddled down. Getting any sleep was nearly impossible, and to make matters worse, since all four of us had contracted food poisoning, we were also filling our living space with vomit, urine, and feces.

Although we were not eating or drinking, I was able to get IVs into my three teammates, providing them with some much needed fluids. Not being medics themselves, they unsuccessfully tried getting a line into me, but all they managed to accomplish for their efforts was to cause a bad infection in my arm around the eight-to-ten unsuccessful sticks.

Our mission was to simply observe and record our findings from our lay-up site, so for the most part we remained quiet, each lost in his own thoughts. We were miserable and the conditions were terrible, but this was something we had all trained for. We knew what we were in for when we were handed this operation and we were prepared to deal with just about anything. After all, we were conducting a secretive mission halfway round the world with almost no one knowing where we were or why we were there. This is exactly the kind of thing that I had joined the SEALs for in the first place, and deep down inside I relished in the challenge.

On our third day in the hole, we spotted movement farther inland and soon identified a thin man dressed in flowing robes and sporting a closely-cropped beard. He was coming directly towards us, although it was obvious that he had no idea that we were there just yet. We quickly rousted one another and within a few seconds each of us was focused on the thin man, our weapons trained on him the entire time. There was a part of me that simply wanted to pull the trigger and eliminate the threat before he inadvertently stumbled across our position, but our rules of engagement clearly stated that we weren't allowed to fire unless we were first fired upon. All we could do was wait and watch as he drew nearer, hoping beyond hope that he might turn in another direction.

When he was about ten meters from our position the man suddenly stopped. He had clearly spotted us in our sand- and sewage-filled hole, despite our desert camouflage netting. His eyes went wide with shock when he realized what he was seeing. We sat completely still for a heartbeat or two before he threw his arms up in the air, turned and fled. He was screaming something in Arabic at the top of his lungs as he sped away, and while we weren't sure exactly what he was saying, we knew that it wasn't good.

Our demolitions raid wasn't scheduled to take place until the following night, but with our hide site compromised, we knew we had to act fast. We waited until after nightfall and then proceeded to start digging up all of the gear we had buried nearby. Our plan was simple: collect all of our equipment, re-inflate the Zodiac, prepare our dive gear, and proceed into the harbor where we would attach a mine to a ship that was the designated target for our raid. We were accelerating the timetable since we were compromised and knew the thin man would no doubt be sending hostile forces our way.

Exhausted from a lack of sleep and weak from not getting enough nutrients, we were eager to be moving again. Under the cover of darkness, three of us went about recovering the buried gear, while the fourth member of the team kept an eye out for approaching enemy personnel. We were just getting our equipment sorted when our teammate on security duty told us in a calm, controlled voice, "guys, put your hands up."

As a SEAL, you never hear anybody tell you to put your hands up, so I immediately knew something was up. We all turned to see what he was talking about and quickly noticed more than a dozen armed gunmen standing behind him with AK-47s pointed in our direction. They looked nervous and unsure of themselves, which can sometimes be a recipe for disaster. We tried to diffuse the situation by standing completely still and raising our hands over our heads while they quickly scrambled to surround us.

Our team only had one weapon at the ready and it was already trained on the gunmen. The other three of us could have dropped our shovels and grabbed our own weapons too, but they would have slaughtered us where we stood. We could have made a break for the water, but they would have easily killed us there as well. We ended up making the right decision by just standing there with our hands in the air.

As they got closer, you could see the fear in their eyes. They were all young and apparently untrained locals, each of whom had a look of nervous panic on their faces. I could see that they all had their fingers on the trigger of their AKs too, which is not a good combination.

What followed was several tense minutes of heated, very loud broken communication with the leader of the gunmen screaming at us in a language none of us understood. He kept motioning to the ground and was trying to get us all to lay down. We tried to communicate to him in English that we were Americans and that we didn't understand what he was saying. At some point, this seemed to register with him, which is when he turned and barked an order at one of his men. That gunman nodded his head and sped off into the night. We just stood there waiting at gunpoint until daylight.

Several hours passed before the gunman burst back onto the scene with another man in tow. The second man spoke a bit of broken English and told us that he was a local merchant who could help translate the conversation. He said that the locals were very angry that we were trespassing on their land and that they wanted us to lay face down on the ground so they could shoot us in the back. He explained very matter of factly that this was how they dealt with trespassers.

We informed him that we weren't about to just lay down and allow ourselves to be shot to death, which initiated a somewhat surprisingly civil discussion that went back and forth for a while. The group leader's temper eventually calmed down as we negotiated, helping to lower the tension level considerably. The gunmen continued to keep their AK-47s aimed at our heads and chests, however, providing a not-so-subtle reminder of just how precarious our situation truly was.

Eventually we were able to convince the leader that we were members of the American military who had gotten lost on a training exercise and accidentally stumbled into his territory. We apologized and promised it wouldn't happen again. He pondered those words for a few moments, then gruffly told us to go, pointing directly at our Zodiac boat. With that, he turned, said a few words to his men, and walked away, with the rest of the group soon following.

A bit dumbfounded, we went about gathering up our gear and preparing to depart. It was at that point that the lieutenant in charge of our four-man squad quietly reminded us that our operation wasn't over yet. We may have avoided being captured and escaped certain death, but we still had a mission to complete. So, without hesitation we donned our wetsuits, collected our equipment, and waded back out into the shark-infested waters, making our way towards the harbor. Time was truly of the essence now, but we still hadn't done what we had come to do.

Over the next twelve hours we waited patiently until dark, then swam into the harbor, located our target, placed explosive charges on its hull, and snuck back to our spot on the beach. By then, the sun was starting to come up once again and we knew we had to make ourselves scarce, as quickly as possible. But, in our rush to complete the operation, we had accidentally anchored the Zodiac in a location that left it high and dry after the tide had gone out. As a result, it was stranded on the sand, far from the water. Before we could go anywhere, we would need to haul it back into the surf, then collect all of the remaining gear. That took several trips to accomplish, all the while we knew that we were quickly running out of time.

Dawn was breaking by the time we fired up the motor on the Zodiac and safely sped back out to sea. At that point, we had already missed our primary pick-up time, which meant we would have to wait at least another twenty-four hours for extraction or make the switch to plan B, which offered an alternate way to get picked up. Ultimately, we elected to go with the second option.

Our contingency plan was to trek for over five hours through the desert then radio HQ that we would be contacting a local guide who could lead us to a nearby landing strip. That airfield would serve as our extraction point, allowing us to finally get on a flight back to Cairo. We met our Ethiopian asset just after nightfall, and he led us to the location as promised. We waited until almost sunrise before paying him and sending him on his way. Then we carefully traversed the airstrip, took cover in nearby brush, and waited some more.

After about an hour a C-130 cargo plane finally appeared overhead, descending towards the runway at a rapid pace. It dropped out of the sky like a flying brick and for a moment it seemed as if it was going to crash into the ground. Then, at the last minute, the pilot pulled up, gently touched down, and slammed on the brakes, creating a cloud of smoke and dust. Just as suddenly, the rear ramp on the plane dropped to the ground and the four of us sprung to our feet and sprinted towards the aircraft in full combat gear. Within a matter of moments we were onboard, the ramp closed behind us, and the aircraft was lifting off once again.

The mission had been a success, but it hadn't been easy. None of us had slept more than an hour or two over the previous four days and we were all still sick, hungry, and dehydrated. Exposure to extreme heat, sandstorms, and sea water had taken its toll, not to mention the tense run-in with some very angry locals.

But through it all, I never worried about whether or not we were going to make it out alive. The men I conducted the mission with were all exceptionally trained professionals who were very good at their jobs. We had been given clear-cut objectives, a plan of action on how to achieve them, and some contingencies should anything go wrong. We also were physically fit—despite contracting food poisoning—and had the right mindset to see us through the grueling obstacles that were put in front of us.

Knowing all of that, I approached the operation with a high level of confidence that not only would we achieve our objectives, we'd also find a way to get back out alive. All of the necessary ingredients were in place and ultimately, we were able to get the job done, despite facing hostile opposition.

Even though we had been pushed to our physical and mental limits, at no time during the mission did we ever even consider quitting. Sick beyond belief, baking in the sun, and sitting in a foxhole filled with our own excrement that continually filled up with sea water, we patiently waited for our chance to conduct the raid. When we were taken prisoner by the tribesmen, we miraculously negotiated our release and when they agreed to let us go, we immediately prepared for the second phase of the mission. Not one of us ever complained about the conditions, or how difficult it was. I was so proud to be with those warriors.

Had we looked for them, we would have found many excuses for quitting. It would have been easy for us to say that we were too sick or too tired to continue. No one would have blamed us if we had bugged out after being held at gunpoint by angry locals. But failure is not something that sits well with me, or any other SEAL, and we weren't about to go home without accomplishing the mission we had come to do. The only excuse that would have allowed us to give up on the operation was if we were dead. All four of us still had a pulse, so the expectation was that we would continue. No excuses.

Of course, that's exactly what Navy SEALs do. And that's exactly what you should do too when defining your own mission in life, no matter where your goals and ambitions take you. Never, ever give up. If you're going through hell, don't slow down. Stay focused on the mission. If you keep advancing towards your goals, a solution to almost every problem will usually present itself. You may not always be able to see it at the time, but hard working, relentlessly driven people with a don't-quit mindset tend to find a way to prevail, no matter the obstacles.

HENRI CHARRIÈRE

Human beings are resilient creatures. We find ways to survive in the harshest environments and in some of the most trying conditions imaginable. Nowhere is this more evident than in the life of Frenchman Henri Charrière, who you might know better by his nickname—Papillon—a reference to the butterfly tattoo he bore on his chest.

Charrière was a safecracker and petty thief who was part of the Paris underworld in the 1920s. In 1931, he was wrongly convicted of murdering a pimp and found himself sentenced to ten years of hard labor in the French penal colony system. This resulted in him getting shipped off to St-Laurent-du-Maroni prison in French Guyana where he was ordered to serve out his time.

Not long after arriving in the prison, Charrière and two other prisoners staged a daring escape and went on the run for several months. Eventually they stole a boat and attempted to sail away to freedom, but ended up shipwrecked along the coast of Colombia, where they were captured and imprisoned. But Papillon had a knack for escaping from confinement and it wasn't long before he had slipped away once again. This time, he journeyed into the jungle where he was adopted by the local indigenous peoples, who allowed him to live with them for a time.

Fearing that he might be caught, Charrière knew that he couldn't stay with his new friends forever. He left his life in the jungle behind and returned to civilization, where he was quickly recognized and recaptured. Upon his return to prison he was given the harshest punishment possible, and was placed in solitary confinement for two very long years.

While he was in solitary another prisoner whom Charrière had befriended found a way to smuggle him extra food and water. When the warden discovered that the former safecracker was getting contraband supplies, he immediately demanded to know who was responsible. Charrière refused to give up his friend's name, prompting the guards to cut his rations in half and close off all light into his cell for six months. Locked away in that tiny cell, with no human contact and no daylight, Papillon was pushed to his absolute limits, resorting to eating insects just to survive.

Two years in solitary would normally be enough to break just about any man, but Charrière was incredibly mentally tough. Upon release, he was sent to the hospital at St-Laurent-du-Maroni to recover, but as soon as he was back on his feet he began looking for ways to escape for a third time. He ended up succeeding on several occasions, although each time he was eventually recaptured and brought back into custody, often serving more time in solitary confinement as a result.

After yet another escape, the warden decided to ship Papillon off to Devil's Island, a penal colony that was home to some of the toughest and most notorious prisoners that came out of France at the time. In fact, French dissidents, political prisoners, and other hard-ened criminals from all over the world were sent to the island, which had a reputation for being completely inescapable. Towering rock cliffs and turbulent seas surrounded the place, making it incredibly difficult for anyone to ever get away.

Never one to back down from a challenge, Charrière began look-ing for ways to get off the island and after spotting a strong tide moving out to sea he hatched a desperate plan. If he could find a way to float out into that current, he might be able to escape one final time. It was a risk he was willing to take if it meant that it might win him his freedom at long last.

Biding his time, Charrière went about collecting coconuts and hiding them away in his cabin. When he had gathered a sufficient number, he placed them all in a bag and sealed it up tight. When all was ready, he carried the bag to the shore, jumped from a high cliff, and plunged into the water below. With the coconuts serving as a makeshift floatation device, he was able to drift out to sea and into the current, which ended up pushing him along for more than three miles, eventually depositing him on a beach in mainland Guyana.

Despite his daring escape, it didn't take long before Charrière was captured and thrown back in prison. This time it was for the final time however and in 1941 he was released at long last. The thief was a free man after spending nearly eleven years in captivity.

Upon release, Charrière settled in Venezuela and created a new life for himself. Eventually he wrote his memoir entitled *Papillon*, which was released in 1969 and went on to sell 1.5 million copies. It was made into a motion picture starring Steve McQueen and Dustin Hoffman in 1973. That same year he would return to Paris for the first time since his incarceration. The following year, he was par-doned of the murder conviction that sent him to prison in the first place, and subsequently cleared of all charges.

Over the course of his time in French Guyana, Papillon escaped from prison on nine separate occasions and spent several stints in solitary confinement. Throughout it all however, he continued to maintain his innocence of the murder charge and was constantly looking for ways to win his freedom.

His story, which some believe is an amalgamation of Charrière's life and that of several other prisoners, remains an inspirational one decades after it was first told. It is a classic display of the indomitable spirit of man, searching for hope when all seems lost, while never giving up on the dream of freedom. It didn't matter what his captors did to him physically—they couldn't break him mentally. His mind never quit, stopped dreaming, or stopped scheming until he was a free man at long last. That is the epitome of Combat Mindset.

Chapter 9

TOUCHING THE LINE

"To succeed, work hard, never give up, and above all cherish a magnificent obsession."

—Walt Disney

I'm a firm believer that in order to truly know where your boundaries lie, you must first push yourself to your very limits, and sometimes even a little further. It is only when you begin to explore the edges of your physical and mental capabilities that you'll actually start to understand all of the things that you are capable of accomplishing; and in doing so, you'll also be able to identify a very important line. It's a line that defines when you're performing at your highest level—your full capacity if you will—and when you you've crossed over into dangerous territory that could potentially end up costing you far more than you ever imagined.

It can be a heady feeling to test your limits and discover your full potential. When you start to realize that you can accomplish great things, you're likely to want to continue exploring those limits even further. This can often lead to continually escalating goals as your expectations of yourself and your objectives change over time. As you grow stronger, more confident, and capable, you should turn those former macro-goals into micro-goals.

That's exactly how it started for me. When I went running for the very first time, I could barely go a couple of miles before I was tired, winded, and wanting to quit. It was a terrible feeling and I was determined to not let it happen again. So I started training, and little by little I improved my speed and endurance. The next time I ran with Dave, I didn't just keep up—I was able to run farther and faster than he did.

After that I was obsessed, and began training for the Boston Marathon, the first of many to come. When I was able to complete that race, I was determined to go faster in my next event. I started looking for other endurance challenges to set my sights on, which ultimately led to ultramarathons, ultra-distance bike races, triathlons, Ironman events, and adventure racing. Even as I pushed myself to new athletic challenges, it seemed I was always looking to the horizon in search of the next big goal to come my way. This led to a never-ending cycle of training, competing, and testing the very limits of my endurance. I ended up racing in over a thousand competitions and learned many lessons along the way. As it turns out, I wasn't just competing in the events, I was competing with myself too. As I set my goals ever-higher, I was constantly comparing my performance with things I had done in the past, pushing myself to go to the next level. The harder, more demanding, or more extreme a race was, the more it appealed to me. As a result, over time I went from spending just a few hours running marathons, to days and weeks in the wilderness competing in extreme adventure races and climbing difficult mountains.

Eventually the regimented training schedule that I set for myself began to take its toll. At one point, while training for the world's longest distance triathlon, I was running over seventy-five miles a week, cycling over three hundred miles a week, swimming over eight miles a week, and lifting weights, all on top of my already demanding day-to-day activities with the SEAL Team. After a while, all of that physical activity started to catch up with me. Although I thought I was in great physical shape, my body was starting to revolt against the demands I continually placed on it. I was pushing myself too hard for too long, well above "the line" and I didn't even realize it.

I remember the commanding officer of SEAL Team ONE asking me one day where the other half of my body was. I had been pushing myself so hard that my body was actually consuming itself for energy. I was fit and fast, but I was very lean, especially for a SEAL.

One summer morning, in Coronado, California, I had just finished a very difficult four-mile workout with the Olympic swim coach who was training me at the time. When I arrived at the pool, a professional female triathlete champion was startled when she looked down at my very swollen feet. She asked why they were so beat up and with so many red marks on them.

The red marks were caused by the eyelets of my running shoes digging into my swollen feet when I ran. Worse yet, the pain pills, which a SEAL Team doctor prescribed to help me manage the inflammation, aches, and pains, had stopped working. My complexion had turned a greenish tint and my face had become very gaunt. When I took a deep breath you could see the veins in my abdomen and chest. I was always cold from being down to less than five percent body fat. My feet, knees, left quadriceps, left shoulder, back, and neck were in constant pain. I was losing a lot of weight and my muscles were being consumed for use as fuel. I was ignoring the warning signs that my body was clearly giving me because I was too busy pursuing my athletic goals.

Everything came to a head one evening when I returned home from my twenty-mile run at a seven-minute pace. I was exhausted and not feeling well but shrugged it off as just being tired. When I came through the door my wife was shocked by my appearance, especially the green tint to my skin. She wanted to call the ambulance, but I explained that I just needed some rest. As I walked down the hallway toward the bed room I ended up passing out, collapsing on the floor in a heap. After I regained consciousness I thought that maybe I should take a bath to help ease the pain, but I was unable to walk to the bathroom since my feet were in terrible agony. I had to crawl to the bathroom on my hands and knees and passed out again before I ever even made it there.

When I came to this time, I found myself in the emergency room. I wasn't exactly sure what had happened or how I got there, but I felt as though I had been run over by a truck. I had bonked hard, but it was by far the worse bonk of my life. Every part of my body hurt and I barely had enough energy to move, talk or focus my eyes on anything. Something was obviously very wrong.

The first voice I heard as I lay on the stretcher in the ER, was from a doctor looking at my feet. I heard him say, "Maybe it was from poisonous insect bites." I was embarrassed to tell him but tried to explain that the marks were not from bug bites but were from the eyelets in my running shoes. They asked how much I was running, and I told them about seventy-five miles a week. I did not go into detail about the additional activities I was doing as part of my training.

The doctor wanted to get some x-rays of my neck, but I was unable to lift my head due to excessive pain at the base of my skull. I tried using my left arm to prop my head up instead, but the pain in my shoulder was so severe that it greatly limited my range of motion. Eventually I managed to use my right hand to lift my head up just enough so a doctor could slide the x-ray plate under my neck.

After a full examination, the doctors determined that I had a wide variety of ailments that included a compressed spine, a torn rotator cuff, and a torn quadricep. I was also suffering from bilateral plantar fascia in my feet, but most serious of all my liver and kidneys were shutting down. This explained my gaunt, greenish complexion. My body was way beyond exhausted, and was also woefully deficient on nutrients it needed to repair itself. I was simply not consuming enough calories to keep up with the pace I had set for myself. The doctor told me it was the worst case of overtraining he had ever seen and that I was literally killing myself.

The only cure was to rest, allow my body to heal, and to ease back on the training for a while. It was a very difficult diagnoses to hear, but it was also an important wake-up call. I had literally pushed myself to the limits of human endurance and then continued well past that line. This would prove to be an important lesson in the future and a constant reminder for myself that it is good to just push yourself far enough that you touch that line, but don't go over it. After that, you can ease off and recover some.

By learning to regulate my training, I could avoid similar breakdowns in the future and actually compete on a higher level over time. By touching the line and not going over it, I could reassure myself I was not leaving a void in my efforts. For more than twenty-two years I trained and worked out every single day. It was a big part of how I defined myself. But over time, I learned to adjust my schedule, to give myself a break here and there. This helped me to avoid burn out, stay healthy, and keep from doing permanent damage to my body and other aspects of my life.

I would never suggest to anyone that they should go over that line themselves. For decades, I felt that if I did not bonk, hallucinate, or "bleed from any orifice," that I was not giving it my all. In hindsight, I was wrong. Now, I am very confident in stating, don't go over that line. It can be extremely dangerous and bad things can result. Simply identify where that line sits, reach for it, touch it, and then back off. That way you can be sure that you are not leaving anything in the proverbial tank without pushing yourself into dangerous territory, where you could bonk hard or do permanent damage.

An obsession with achieving your goals can be very rewarding when chasing hard to reach objectives. The focus that comes along with it can serve as the motivating factor that allows you to reach the goals that you've set for yourself. But when that obsession becomes all-consuming, it can rule your life to the point where nothing else matters, including your health, mental well-being, or relationships with others. Whether you're spending long days at the office or you're out training for a competition, it is important to keep things in perspective and foster the relationships with those around you. Finding the balance between pursuing your goals and maintaining a normal lifestyle can be difficult, but it is an important part of staying physically and mentally fit.

The reality is overtraining is a common issue for many endurance athletes. There is a certain level of discomfort and pain that comes along with any type of physical training and the ability to ignore those issues can be a real asset while preparing for—or competing in—a race. But, it can also lead to the types of problems that I encountered when I ended up almost killing myself by pushing well beyond my limits. It can also be incredibly counterproductive, causing a feeling of being sluggish and fatigued all of the time, and ultimately causing performance levels to plateau or drop rather than continue to improve. In other words, you're better off pushing yourself as hard as you can and then backing off, because in the long run, it is a much better approach to getting ready for race day, while also safeguarding your overall well-being.

Knowing when to back off, take a break, and rest is crucial, whether you're competing in a sporting event, launching a new business, or just learning a new skill. Focusing too long and too hard on a single objective can lead to burn out, which can be detrimental to long-term success. A lot of people fail to reach their full potential simply because they jump headlong into a project, immerse themselves completely in reaching their goal, and end up never completing it simply because they expend all of their energy just getting started. They literally run out of gas and can't seem to find a way to pace themselves to the finish line.

Doggedly pursuing your goals isn't a bad thing in and of itself. Often times, the person who finds the most success in life is the one who thinks about how to reach his or her goals and is laser-focused on making that happen. The difference is, they also seem to find a way to pace themselves throughout the journey. The key here is once again identifying the thin line between pushing yourself too far and crashing and burning, as opposed to simply touching that line and then easing back long enough to recover and carry on.

So how exactly do you know where that line is? It is different for each of us, but usually you'll be able to tell if you pay attention to some important cues. Exhaustion, irritability, having difficulty concentrating, headaches, and other bodily pains are often associated with the stress that comes with overwork and overtraining. Recognizing those symptoms and easing back is often the most challenging part.

In my case, my body was telling me it needed a break, but I just didn't listen to it. I was exhausted, I wasn't recovering properly, and I was well beyond the end of my rope. Had I paid attention to those warning signs and allowed myself to back off from my intense workout schedule, I could have avoided the fallout that came with overtraining altogether. This would have allowed me to compete in that ultra-triathlon I was preparing for, rather than spending time as a patient in a hospital.

Despite the fact that many endurance athletes tend to over train from time to time, that doesn't seem to be an issue for mountaineers. Instead, mountaineers run the risk of suffering from something called "summit fever," which is an obsession that is equally compelling and perhaps even more dangerous.

By it's purest definition, summit fever is a compulsion that pushes climbers to continue climbing with the single goal of reaching the top of the mountain, no matter the circumstances or the costs. It can manifest both in people who are completely new to the sport or the very experienced. It usually strikes at a time when the alpinist knows he or she should turn back due to safety concerns, but they press on nonetheless. Often times they believe that the summit is closer than it actually is or they're moving faster than they actually are. They operate under the delusion that if they just continue climbing, they'll eventually reach their goal.

Summit fever has been cited as the cause of many deaths in the mountains and played a crucial role in the 1996 Everest disaster as chronicled in Jon Krakauer's classic book *Into Thin Air* (1997). Over the course of a few days, eight people lost their lives when an unexpected and incredibly dangerous storm descended upon the mountain. Many of those lives could have been saved had they not been so focused on reaching the summit of the world's highest peak.

In the early 1990s, New Zealand mountain guide Rob Hall was one of the top climbers on Everest, playing a crucial role in opening it up to commercial expeditions. At the time of the disaster, he was leading a group of clients who had paid a significant amount of money to be on the mountain just to get a crack at its elusive summit. One of those clients was a man named Doug Hansen, who had come to Everest the previous year with Hall but hadn't managed to summit. Hansen knew that after spending tens of thousands of dollars on his venture that it could be his last opportunity to climb the mountain, and as a result he had decided he was getting to the top no matter what.

When climbing a mountain like Everest, expedition leaders

typically set a turn-around time. If alpinists haven't reached the summit by that prearranged time of day, they are required to turn around and head back down. This is for their own safety as well as the safety of the entire climbing team. It helps to ensure they have plenty of time to descend back to camp while its still daylight, and they have enough oxygen, food, and water for the descent. On May 10, 1996, Hall had set this deadline for turning back as 2:00 p.m.

That day the Everest guide was leading his team up the South Col on the Nepali side of the mountain. While making the ascent, a series of delays caused the group to move slower than Hall had anticipated. On more than one occasion they even had to wait for a team of Sherpas to install climbing ropes on some of the steeper sections. Eventually they were able to get moving again, but time was starting to run out. The team needed to pick up the pace or they could end up summiting too late in the day. Worse yet, storm clouds were gathering on the horizon, threatening to change the weather dramatically.

A number of the climbers on Hall's team reached the summit safely and started back down prior to the 2:00 p.m. deadline. But Hansen was moving very slowly and struggling to keep pace. At one point, he came across a Sherpa named Ang Dorje (who I had the good fortune to climb with on Everest two decades later). Ang reminded Hansen of the turn-around time and ordered him to start back down, but the American climber wasn't about to give up on his dream, particularly when he was so close to reaching the top. Consumed by summit fever the idea of turning back while he was just a few hundred feet from his goal was unthinkable.

Eventually, Hall arrived on the scene and told Ang Dorje to continue descending to their campsite, indicating that he would personally escort Hansen to the top. This was completely out of character for Hall, who knew the risks that they faced better than almost anyone. Having stood on the summit of Everest four times in the past, it seemed unlikely that he'd be caught up in summit fever of his own. Nevertheless, he made the decision to continue upwards with his client in tow. The two men eventually reached the highest point on the planet around 4:00 p.m., well past the predetermined turn-around time.

By that point, the storm that had been forming on the horizon

was barreling down on the mountain, bringing a full-fledged bliz-
zard, much colder temperatures, and high winds with it. Hansen and
Hall tried to descend in the quickly-deteriorating conditions, but the
weather just kept getting worse. They would end up seeking shelter
on a shallow ledge in an attempt to wait out the storm, but due to the
plummeting temperatures, the extreme altitude, and raging winds,
both men ended up perishing on Everest.

Hansen's summit fever compelled him to go upwards even when
he knew he needed to turn back. Hall, who knew better than to
push his luck on a dangerous 8,000-meter peak, was caught up in
Hansen's obsession too and even though he should have stuck to his
own strict rules, he accompanied his client to the top. It was a fatal
mistake for both men and it could have easily been avoided.

Turning back wasn't a sign of weakness or failure; it was simply a matter of knowing when they were pushing themselves beyond
acceptable limits. The turn-back time is standard mountaineering
protocol for a reason, but Hansen and Hall chose to ignore it and
continue on anyway. Had they recognized that they were crossing
over the line they both could have made it back down safely and returned to climb Everest another day.

Polish alpinist Wanda Rutkiewicz is another climber who let
summit fever and obsession with reaching her goals cloud her judge-
ment, eventually leading to her death. In the late 1970s and early
'80s, Wanda was a rising star in the mountaineering world, knocking off an impressive string of achievements that included her becoming just the third woman to summit Everest and the first to climb K2.

After finding success on some of the toughest and tallest mountains on the planet, Rutkiewicz decided to set a major goal for herself, announcing her intentions to become the first woman to climb
all fourteen of the world's 8,000-meter peaks. At that point in her
career, only a handful of men had been able to accomplish that feat.
Climbing those massive mountains was—and still is—the gold standard by which high altitude mountaineers are measured.

By 1990, Rutkiewicz had managed to knock off six of those big
mountains, adding Nanga Parbat, Shishapangma, and Gasherbrum
I and II to her resume. That left her with eight peaks to go before

reaching her goal. It was about then that she came up with an ambitious plan called the "Caravan of Dreams," which would allow her to complete those eight remaining mountains over the course of a single year. It was incredibly audacious and left very little room for error.

In the months that followed, she climbed Cho Oyu and Annapurna before turning her sights on a 28,169-foot mountain in Nepal called Kangchenjunga. Its peak is the third highest in the world and a significant technical challenge, too. Getting to the top is no easy feat, but with her years of experience and raw natural talent Rutkiewicz was more than up to the task.

On May 12, 1992, climber Carlos Carsolio met Rutkiewicz about three hundred meters below the summit. He had been climbing with her, but she was moving very slowly, and as a result he ended up reaching the summit without her. When they met, she was preparing to bivouac in a snow cave for the night and was planning on making her final summit push the following morning. Knowing that she had already been in the thin air of the "death zone" for many hours and had ignored her own turn-around time, Carsolio urged her to return to their camp at lower altitude. The Polish woman wasn't properly equipped and didn't even have a sleeping bag, tent, a stove, or fuel, and was running low on food and water. She also seemed to be suffering from the early stages of altitude sickness, which didn't bode well for her chances. Rutkiewicz refused to descend however, saying she would stay where she was and go to the top the following day. That was the last time anyone would ever see her alive.

Rutkiewicz's comrade descended back to Camp 2 and remained on the mountain for several days waiting for her return. She never came down however and her friends and family would be left to wonder what became of her in those final hours of her life. It was a devastating loss for the mountaineering community and for the entire country of Poland, which deeply mourned her passing.

I never had the privilege of meeting Rutkiewicz, however my good friend and climbing teacher Jay Smith—a legendary expedition leader in his own right—was a good friend of Wanda and had great respect for her. By most accounts, Rutkiewicz was a force of nature who was strong willed, physically imposing, and extremely confident in her own abilities. This often led to conflicts with other climbers, who didn't always appreciate her brash attitude or couldn't measure up to the high standards that she set for herself and those around her. It also led to relationship problems, as she single-mindedly pursued her goal of climbing all of the 8,000-meter peaks at the expense of just about every other aspect of her life. Because she was gone for extended periods of time her personal relationships—not to mention her finances—often suffered. Despite being a world-class mountaineer, she routinely left a path of destruction in her wake as she obsessively pursued her climbing goals.

The exact fate of the Polish climber remains a mystery and what happened on Kangchenjunga in those final hours will likely never be known. But had she not been caught in the grip of summit fever, she would have been able to make better decisions, ones that may have sent her safely down the mountain where she could have lived to climb another day. Instead, Rutkiewicz saw the choice as one of success versus failure, and since failure wasn't an option, she decided to continue her climb, even though the level of danger was unacceptably high. In the mountaineering community it is often said that "reaching the summit is optional, getting down is mandatory."

Often times, while pursuing a goal, we tend to see things in shades of black and white just as Rutkiewicz had. We perceive our options to be either success or failure, even though that is seldom the case. Rarely do we have only one or two choices when it comes to navigating our way through the challenges we're confronted with in pursuit of our goals. Knowing when to back off, give ourselves a break, and allow ourselves to recover can play a crucial role in terms of our long-term success. This is just as true for endurance athletes as it is for businessmen and women, entrepreneurs, mountaineers, and pretty much everyone else for that matter.

The concept of summit fever may have originated in the mountaineering community, but it can be applied to a wide variety of aspects of our lives. Becoming consumed with achieving a very specific goal is something that can happen to just about anyone, whether they are training for a competition, closing a business deal, or designing some revolutionary new product. A healthy amount of obsession can be the driving force needed to find success, but as always, too much of a good thing can also keep you from reaching your objectives. Even in the SEAL Teams, you'll hear guys often say "too much can do can do you in." That's why most training programs have runners easing up on their workouts as they get closer to the race and why even the busiest and most successful business executives need to take a vacation on occasion.

The confidence and mental toughness that comes along with achieving micro-goals is a good thing, helping us to push our own physical and mental boundaries in pursuit of our larger, macro-goals. But, that same sense of confidence can also cause us to overestimate our abilities at times, which can end up leading to trouble. Because of this it is important to remain hyper-vigilant of the warning signs that come with pushing yourself, your team, or your family too hard for too long. If you're physically exhausted, having trouble sleeping, finding your immune system compromised regularly, or you're seeing a sudden drop in performance, it may be an indication that you've pushed yourself over the line and have stayed there for too long.

Simply put, the human body can accomplish amazing things and is far more resilient and complex than we often give it credit for. But when it is over-worked and pushed too hard for too long, it will break down, and can leave us completely devastated as a result. Such was the case with British polar explorer Henry Worsley, whose tale is certainly a cautionary one.

A career army officer, Worsley was a member of the UK's Special Air Service with tours of duty in Afghanistan, Northern Ireland, Kosovo, and Bosnia. But his true passion was exploring the Antarctic, a place that he had visited on more than one occasion. In 2012, he successfully skied more than 870 miles to the South Pole in celebration of the one-hundredth anniversary of the epic duel between Amundsen and Scott to be the first to reach that same point a century earlier.

Gripped by his love for Antarctica, Worsley returned in November of 2015 with an even more ambitious goal. He wanted to become the first person to traverse the continent completely unas- sisted while on foot. Others had made the journey before, although it was always with some additional means of transportation, including motorized vehicles, dogsleds, or large kites that could harness the wind to pull them along across the surface. Worsley wanted to make the journey under his own power however, without any outside help or even teammates to keep him company.

The journey would begin at a place called Berkner Island and would end on the Ross Ice Shelf, covering some 950 miles with a brief stopover at the South Pole along the way. To cover that distance without outside assistance Worsley would need to drag a sled weighing nearly three hundred pounds behind him at all times. That sled contained all of the supplies and equipment required to survive in the harsh Antarctic environment, including fuel, food, cold weather gear, and satellite communication devices.

In the early going, Worsley struggled to "find his legs," which is common for polar explorers at the start of an expedition. The heavy sled, poor weather conditions, and cold temperatures take some time to adjust to. But as the days wore on, the British Army officer started to find his rhythm, increasing both his speed and distance. It wasn't long before he was covering respectable chunks of mileage each day, despite the ongoing challenges that he faced.

Still, crossing the Antarctic takes time and over the course of the next two months the expedition turned into a real grind. The endless days out on the ice started to take their toll on Worsley's body and as he inched towards the finish line, his progress began to slow. He had pushed himself to his absolute limits and it was getting harder and harder for him to even crawl out of his sleeping bag each morning. Packing up his tent and other gear then skiing ten to twelve hours became increasingly harder as the explorer's energy waned.

As his progress continued to slow a new concern arose. Would Henry be able to reach the extraction point for his expedition before the austral summer came to an end? Travel in the Antarctic is only possible during the warmest months of the year, which run from the start of November to the end of January. That deadline was fast approaching, which meant a change in weather was coming, too. Despite how difficult the conditions had been up until that point, they would get a lot worse once the Antarctic summer ended.

Still, Worsley soldiered on as best he could until one day he simply found that he didn't have the strength to get up and start moving. He lay there in his tent, nestled inside of his sleeping bag, unable to move. His body was exhausted beyond belief and he knew he needed to give it time to rest. So he told himself he'd take the day off, recover some energy, and resume his journey the following day. But that day came and went as well, and he still couldn't manage to get up and get moving.

Finally, on day seventy-one of the expedition, Henry used his satellite phone to call for help. With time running short and his body completely exhausted, he knew it was time to give up and go home. He had traveled a total of 913 miles and was just thirty miles short of finishing, a distance that would have taken him just two or three more days to complete were he healthy and feeling better. But he simply didn't have the energy required to press on.

As soon as Worsley's call for assistance came in, a search and rescue team was dispatched to retrieve him from the ice. They loaded the explorer and his gear onto a plane and flew him back to Punta Arenas, Chile where he was immediately admitted to a hospital to begin treatment for severe dehydration and exhaustion. While there, doctors discovered that Henry was also suffering from bacterial peritonitis, an infection that can cause swelling of the abdomen, nausea, vomiting, and a lack of energy. Left untreated the affliction can even turn the body septic. Emergency surgery was performed on the explorer, but despite the best efforts of the medical staff his organs began to shut down. A short time later Henry succumbed to his ailments and he passed away.

Worsley put in a herculean effort in his attempt to cross the Antarctic unassisted. In doing so, he pushed his body to its absolute limit and as a result he ended up paying the ultimate price. He was so focused on reaching the finish line that he didn't consider what kind of toll the expedition was taking on him physically until it was too late. Had he recognized the signs earlier, he could have pulled the plug on the journey, called for an evacuation sooner, and likely would have survived. Doing so would have meant admitting defeat, but he also would have lived to return home to his family and possibly even given the Antarctic crossing another go at a future date.

As a Special Forces soldier and experienced polar explorer, Worsley no doubt knew his own limits. But he was so determined to see his expedition through to the end that he pushed himself over the line and stayed there for far too long. This left him so physically depleted that he had no choice but to halt his expedition, which must have been a painful decision considering he was so close to achieving his goal.

It is easy to get tunnel vision when we're focused in on a singular objective. Often times we want it so badly that we are willing to sacrifice other important things in our lives in order to get what we want. That isn't a bad thing in and of itself, but when those sacrifices begin to impact our health and relationships, it is time to take a step back and reassess our priorities. Finding the balance between pursuing our goals and pushing too far is the key, because even though achieving our objectives is important and rewarding in its own right, doing so at the expense of our own well-being—or that of those around us—is a pyrrhic victory at best.

Throughout the course of this book we've talked about the importance of mental toughness and tapping into your own inner strength. Recognizing when you've pushed too far and learning to throttle back on the pursuit of your goals takes a certain kind of strength, too. It isn't always easy to accept our own limitations, even when they're staring us directly in the face. But embracing those limitations and learning to work within them is just as important as discovering how far we can push ourselves. With it comes an unexpected strength.

There is a fine line between reaching our full potential and moving into the danger zone, where things get truly serious. Learning to manage that line and use it to your advantage will allow you to accomplish just about anything you set your mind to. Sometimes you'll need to dig deep and push past those boundaries in order to get what you want, but in doing so, it is important to be aware of the dangers you could face along the way. Otherwise, we run the risk of damaging ourselves and those around us in ways that could leave deep and lasting scars, both mental and physical.

You don't have to be an endurance athlete, mountaineer, or explorer to get caught up in the throes of obsession. Few people have left their mark on modern technology and society in the way that Steve Jobs has. As the co-founder of Apple Computers, Jobs is responsible for making seismic shifts in multiple industries, including personal computing, music, movies, telecommunications, and digital publishing. To many, he is a genius who has revolutionized the way we communicate in the twenty-first century. But, for those who worked closely with him he was also incredibly difficult and demanding, often to the point of shredding personal relationships in order to get what he wanted.

Jobs's single-minded pursuit of creating products that were as close to perfection as possible is legendary. He would work long hours—often for days on end—obsessing over every detail to ensure that some new device or piece of software met his exacting standards. He'd also expect his team at Apple to do the same, requiring key members of his staff to be available twenty-four hours a day, seven days a week.

According to many who knew him well, Jobs was a very difficult man to work for. He would impose strict deadlines, set almost-impossible standards, and do everything within his power to coerce his design and engineering teams into achieving his vision; this included everything from praising them for their hard work to berating them for their mistakes, often offering brutal critiques in front of their colleagues.

There is no question that Jobs is one of the most successful businessmen of all time. To achieve this level of success he not only learned how to push himself to his highest levels but push those around him too. That's a skill that many great leaders exhibit across a wide variety of industries, the military, politics, and other cross sections of society. However, Jobs was notorious for doing so in such a way that it left many of his collaborators and coworkers feeling bitter, alienated, and under appreciated, particularly in the early years of his career.

While he always had a reputation for being difficult, Jobs cemented that status while creating the Macintosh computer in the early 1980s. His brash attitude, impossible demands, and ability to completely belittle the engineering team caused many rifts. Worse yet, Jobs was battling Apple CEO John Scully over the future of the company at the same time and was prone to throwing tantrums when things didn't go his way. Ultimately, Scully and the board forced Jobs out of the company he helped create, finding him to be more of a liability than an asset.

In the years that followed, Jobs created another computer company called NeXT, purchased Pixar from *Star Wars* director George Lucas, and pursued a number of other personal projects. During that time he also seemed to gain some perspective about his tenure at Apple and his unceremonious departure. And while he continued to work extremely hard and be incredibly demanding of his team, he also learned to work with them better.

In 1997, Apple bought NeXT and Jobs returned to the fold of his original company. Before long, he was reinstated as CEO and in the years that followed he managed to take it from an organization that was on the verge of bankruptcy to the most valuable company on the planet. It was a remarkable turnaround both for the man and for Apple itself, both of which had seemed like they were teetering on the brink of irrelevance at various points over the previous decade.

During Jobs's second tenure, Apple would see a string of unprecedented successes including the iMac, iPod, and iPhone, a gadget that would become the single biggest consumer electronic device ever created. That one product turned Apple into a global powerhouse, revolutionized the cell phone market and helping to create the mobile computing field.

To produce this string of new successes Jobs remained the same demanding, difficult, and at times, tyrannical boss that he had always been. But those that knew him best say that he also showed a softer side. That he learned to work better with those around him, and while he still insisted that employees give nothing less than 100 percent, he wasn't quite so abrasive and caustic when dealing with them.

It seems that during his years in exile from Apple Jobs learned a lot about himself and the people around him. That didn't change his expectations of himself or his team, but it did give him some insights into how to work more efficiently with others. Jobs's obsession with perfectionism and creating life-changing products never went away, but his approach to achieving those things may have altered some as he gained a bit of perspective.

Steve Jobs wasn't an endurance athlete or an explorer mapping the remote corners of the planet. Nevertheless, he was constantly setting monumental goals for himself and Apple, all the while finding ways to achieve them. Along the way, he was pushing through boundaries of a completely different kind, not the least of which were the expectations of the world around him. To do that, he was also continually pushing himself to defy those expectations and deliver groundbreaking products. In a way, that is a grueling race of a completely different kind.

In order to create the unparalleled string of successes that became his legacy, Jobs had to operate at an incredibly high level on a consistent basis. That means he was functioning on or near that all-important line nearly all of the time. That alone is enough to have a negative impact on your health and relationships, even if it doesn't involve running ultramarathons or skiing to the South Pole.

Considering the strained connections he had with a number of former friends, colleagues, business partners, and family, it is probably safe to say that by focusing on achieving his goals in the manner that he did there was plenty of damage left in his wake. Was it worth it? Only Jobs could have answered that question, but it is good to know that he did repair some of those relationships in the years prior to his death in 2011.

Being able to operate at a consistently high level will certainly allow you to achieve great things and pursue your passions. However, being able to ease back on the throttle from time to time will help you to find and maintain balance in the other areas of your life that are important too. At the end of the day, it doesn't matter how much you've achieved or how impressive your goals are if you don't have anyone to share them with or you're so worn-down, beat-up, and exhausted that you can't appreciate the accomplishment.

Simply put, identify that line, touch it, and then back off and reassess. In the end, productive results can be achieved without causing damage and can make everything else that you've accomplished that much more meaningful.

JANE GOODALL
Conservationist

One of the most well-known personalities of the twentieth century, Jane Goodall is a perfect example of someone who has a knack for pushing herself beyond boundaries. For nearly sixty years, she has studied wild chimpanzees in Africa while advocating for the protection of those creatures. During that time, she has helped us to understand these primates better, while also learning a little bit about ourselves as humans along the way.

Born in 1934 in London, Goodall was raised in a suburban environment far from the wilds of Africa that she would eventually call home. At a young age, her father gave her a stuffed toy chimpanzee that she named "Jubilee," which became one of her favorite possessions. It may have also started her fascination with primates and other wild animals as well because even at a young age Jane dreamed of visiting Africa and spotting wildlife in its natural habitat. That dream would eventually come true, defining her life's work.

In 1957, Goodall got her wish and traveled to Kenya where she met with famed anthropologist Louis Leakey, who had been conducting research on the evolution of man in East Africa for more than three decades. That meeting would be a fateful one for young Jane, with Leakey playing an instrumental role in the direction that her life would take. It was Leakey that arranged for Goodall to study primates with experts back in London, even though she had no formal training in the field. In fact, she didn't even have an undergraduate degree.

After obtaining a minimal amount of training in London, Goodall returned to Africa in 1960 and was sent at Leakey's behest to Gombe Stream National Park in Tanzania. She was instructed to observe the chimpanzee families that lived there and take notes on their behaviors. Without any real formal training however, Jane took an unconventional approach to her field study. For instance, rather than simply giving the chimps a number as a form of reference and recognition like most biologists of the day would have, she gave them names instead. This made them far more relatable to her and helped her to connect with them on a deeper level. The result was a groundbreaking study that revealed aspects of primate behavior that had never been noted before.

Goodall's study would become one of the most important animal research projects of the twentieth century and proved eye-opening to scientists and the general public alike. While observing the chimpanzees at Gombe Stream she discovered two very important things. First, the chimps were capable of using simple tools in their day-to-day tasks and they were not vegetarians as previously thought. The primates were instead omnivores who would occasionally eat meats. Jane also observed aggressive behavior in the animals that had never been recorded before as well, including the hunting of other monkeys and rival chimp families waging war on one another.

The research study's findings were a revelation in many ways, eventually turning Goodall into a celebrity known the world over. By virtue of literally writing the book on chimpanzees, she became the foremost expert on the creatures, which allowed her to skip over undergraduate school altogether and earn a PhD in ethology from Cambridge University. Her thesis covered the chimps that she had come to know so very well while in the field in Tanzania.

What followed was an even more ambitious research project that spanned over fifty years. Much of that research has been supported by the Jane Goodall Institute, which was founded in 1977. That organization was created to not only continue the study of the Gombe chimps, but also to help promote conservation efforts. Goodall has made it her goal to help protect not only the primates that have played such a crucial role in her life, but other animals and endangered habitats in other parts of the world too.

Today, Jane Goodall spends less time actually observing the

chimpanzees and is focused far more on her conservation efforts, which keep her traveling and lecturing at a hectic pace. She works with a number of organizations across the globe with ongoing environmental protection efforts, while also interacting with young people on ways that they can help preserve the planet.

One of the things that makes Goodall's story so impressive is that even at a young age she knew exactly what she wanted to do with her life and was determined to find a way to make it a reality. Her goal was to get to Africa and she was completely focused on finding a way to do just that. At the age of eighteen she took a job as a secretary in London with the hopes of raising the money she needed to make the move to Kenya. It took her four years to do it, but eventually she made it happen. Once there, she met Louis Leakey, became his assistant, and eventually convinced him that she was the right person to conduct the study of chimpanzees in Tanzania.

In 1960, the jungles of Africa were hardly a place for a young woman. Female researchers conducting a study alone in the wild was highly unusual and potentially dangerous. But Goodall was determined to stick it out for as long as she could. At first, things didn't go as planned, as the chimpanzees shied away from her and adapting to the jungle took time. But eventually the chimps came to accept her presence, allowing her to observe them more closely than anyone else had ever done before.

There were so many times throughout her career that Goodall could have given up. Not having enough money to go to college could have sent her down a very different path in life, and yet she still stayed focused on finding her way to Africa. Once there, she had to earn the trust of Leakey, which took several years to accomplish. And when she was sent into the field all alone, the wild setting would have been enough to deter most people from staying for very long. But this was her dream and she wasn't about to let any of those things stand in her way after she had worked so hard to get there.

Goodall was able to take her childhood fascination with wild animals and turn it into a highly successful career that has spanned nearly six decades. Along the way, she has shifted the way we look at primates and how they relate to human beings. She has also managed to inspire generations of other women who have followed her, demonstrating that determination, dedication, and passion can allow you to achieve the things you want most in life.

Even now, well into her eighties, Goodall doesn't seem to be slowing down much. She is proof that we can continue to set and pursue big goals at any stage of our lives. While most people her age are happy to have settled into retirement, she's still searching for ways to continue changing the world, making it a better place not only for the chimps that she loves so much, but for the rest of us as well.

Chapter 10

IT'S NEVER TOO LATE
TO GET STARTED

"You only live once, but if you do it right, once is enough."
                                                        –Mae West

Perhaps the most common excuse most people have for not pursuing their goals is that they are too old or they've waited too long to get started. They often lament the fact that they didn't do the things that they really wanted to do when they were younger and they tell themselves that their window of opportunity has now closed, so what is the point of even trying? Instead, they continue to go about their everyday lives, often wondering about what could have been, as a nagging voice in the back of their brain continues to ask "what if?"

This is yet another excuse that we give ourselves to not pursue the projects and goals that we've always dreamed of, whether that's running a marathon, starting a business, or traveling the world. If you push through your own personal boundaries and believe in yourself, it is never too late. You can achieve great things at any phase of your life, provided you're willing to bet on yourself and are prepared to take a leap of faith.

In the military you often see slogans on shirts and banners that say things like "Pain Builds Character" and "Pain is Good and Extreme Pain is Extremely Good." As we've said before, there are actually two types of pain. The temporary pain of discipline that comes from truly pushing yourself in pursuit of a goal, and the permanent pain of regret that come from quitting or never having tried at all. We all have dreams and aspirations, but our willingness to actually make those ambitions a reality is ultimately what defines us and our legacy.

Now, more than ever, the opportunities to achieve great things can come at virtually any stage of life. People are running marathons well into their seventies, eighties, and beyond. Individuals are embracing new technologies that give them the chance to learn new skills, change careers later in life, and create a lasting legacy that can go well beyond their own lifespan. By realizing that age is just a number and that we are only limited by our perceptions of what that number means, we can set aside the notion that it is never too late to start doing the things that matter to us most. Instead, we can focus on actually getting started on chasing after our goals, no matter how big or small they might be.

Throughout the course of this book we have used running a marathon as a frequent example of how to set a macro-goal and use a series of micro-goals to actually achieve it. The classic marathon remains a universally recognized test of fitness, determination, and focus. But, just because it is a physically demanding activity doesn't mean that it is reserved only for the young.

Fauja Singh is proof of this. Born in Punjab, India in 1911, he was a runner in his youth, but gave up the sport as he grew older. For decades he lived his life as many of us do, going to work each day, raising a family, and devoting his time to his community. This often left him little spare time for his own pursuits and hobbies as he focused on supporting those around him instead.

In the early 1990s Singh lost his wife, a son, and a daughter, over the course of just a few short years. This was a sharp reminder of just how short and precious life can be, as it often slips away before we even realize it. But instead of wallowing in his grief, he turned to running to serve as both therapy and fitness. He was eighty-one years old when he took up the sport for a second time.

In the years that followed, Singh moved to London where he continued to run regularly. It was there that he learned what a marathon actually was, and soon set a goal for himself to take part in a race. He ended up running in the London Marathon in 2000 at the age of eighty-nine, and four years later he would make headlines by completing another race in an impressive five hours and forty minute—faster than many runners half his age.

In October of 2011, Singh did something no one else had ever done before. He completed a marathon at the age of one hundred. While competing in an event held in Toronto he covered the full 26.2-mile course in eight hours and eleven minutes. Unfortunately, he was denied a Guinness World Record because he was unable to produce a birth certificate confirming his age. Such documents just didn't exist in India back in the early twentieth century. But Singh didn't mind—he wasn't running to set records anyway.

Singh continued to run competitively through 2013, at which time he retired from racing altogether. He didn't hang up his running shoes completely however, as he still found time to take part in charity events and hit the street regularly to keep in shape. Running had become such an important part of his life that he simply couldn't let it go completely.

If an Indian Sikh can discover the joys of running, and accept the challenges of training for a marathon in his eighties, many of us can probably do the same. Fauja Singh didn't think that he was too old or that it was too late to start racing; he simply knew that he wanted to run and he wasn't going to let anything keep him from doing just that.

Even those with a long and distinguished resume filled with achieving big goals can still find new challenges later in their lives too. Sir Ranulph Fiennes began his career by serving in the British military, where he was part of the Special Air Service during the 1960s. The SAS is a Special Forces unit in the British Army similar to the US Navy SEALs. He was part of the military for eight years and then left the service to pursue other opportunities.

After his discharge, Fiennes became a professional explorer, joining a team of fellow adventurers on an expedition up the White Nile in Africa by hovercraft. Later, he would lead another team into Iran, where they discovered an ancient lost city hidden in the desert.

But perhaps his biggest accomplishment was the completion of the Transglobe Expedition, which took place from 1979 to 1982. During that adventure, Fiennes and two other former members of the SAS circumnavigated the globe north-to-south, via both the North and South Poles. It was such a major undertaking that no one had ever done it before, nor has anyone repeated the grueling journey since.

Fiennes exploits have earned him the moniker "the world's greatest living explorer" along with an appointment to the Order of the British Empire, earning him the right to add "Sir" to the front of his name. With such an impressive list of accomplishments on his resume, no one would blame him if he had decided to go into retirement, seeking peace and solitude after many years in the field. But that isn't what happened. Not by a long shot.

In 2003, at the age of fifty-nine, Sir Ran completed seven marathons in seven days, on seven different continents. That challenge came just four months after he suffered a massive heart attack and underwent double bypass surgery. A few years later, he would overcome a long-standing fear of heights to scale the North Face of the Eiger, one of the most iconic and technical rock climbs in the world. He would follow up that achievement in 2009 by becoming the oldest Brit to summit Mt. Everest, reaching the top of the world's highest peak at the age of sixty-five.

Obviously Fiennes has always had an adventurous streak, not to mention an uncanny ability to set monumental goals and find a way to achieve them. But, he is also the perfect example of a person who clearly has far too many things that he wants to accomplish in a single lifetime. He is the kind of man who will likely never think that it is too late to start a new project, no matter how big or small. Instead he is more likely to be worried about whether or not he'll have enough time to do all of the things he wants to do before his time on planet Earth comes to an end.

One of the more legendary stories about this larger-than-life explorer is how he lost several fingers on his left hand. In 2000, Fiennes attempted to travel solo and unsupported on foot to the North Pole. Many consider this to be the single most challenging expedition in the world, requiring strength, stamina, and an iron will. At one point during the journey the sleds that he was using to carrying his supplies broke through the ice, plunging into the Arctic Ocean below. Eventually, Fiennes was able to retrieve the lost sleds and the gear they carried, but in doing so he also managed to contract severe frostbite in his hands due to exposure to the frigid waters. Because of this, he had to abandon the expedition altogether and return home.

Upon arriving back in the UK, a doctor examined the explorer's hands and determined that he should wait to see how the skin healed before deciding whether or not any amputations would be necessary. But the pain that Fiennes felt while waiting for the skin to regenerate became unbearable at times, and the impulsive adventurer was impatient to have the healing process behind him. So, one day he went to his own tool shed and used a saw to cut off the injured digits himself. For a man who had already suffered greatly in the pursuit of his goals, cutting off his own fingers was simply something that needed to be done in order to get on with planning his next endeavor.

Fiennes isn't alone in these kinds of adventurous ambitions. Polish kayaker Aleksander Doba is an ageless wonder as well, completing some of the toughest and most demanding expeditions of the twenty-first century so far. In 2010, Doba rose to prominence in the long-distance rowing community when he made a solo crossing of the Atlantic Ocean in a kayak at the age of sixty-five. It took him nearly ninety-nine days to complete the traverse, which began in Dakar in Northern Africa and ended when he reached Brazil in South America.

Three years later, the Polish paddler crossed the Atlantic under his own power for a second time, setting off from Lisbon, Portugal and ending at Smyrna Beach in Florida. That route took Doba across the widest part of the ocean, covering more than 6,300 miles along the way. He ended up spending 196 days aboard his ocean-going kayak, completely alone out on the water the entire time.

Not content to have two successful ocean crossings on his kayaking resume, in 2017 Doba launched yet another attempt to paddle across the Atlantic. This time he decided to travel west-to-east, starting along the coast of New Jersey in the US and ending in Le Conquet, France. That voyage turned out to be much more challenging than he had anticipated, with heavy storms and rough waters often slowing progress to a crawl. On his third journey across the ocean, he spent 110 days at sea, turning seventy-one just one week after he arrived in Europe.

While paddling solo across an ocean is an impressive feat at any age, perhaps Doba's most admirable quality is his tenacity. In 2016, he launched his first attempt to paddle from the US to Europe, but just hours into the expedition, high winds and heavy surf pushed his boat back onto shore, damaging it in the process. For many, that would have been a sign to give up on the journey altogether. But in Doba's case it simply forced him to return to land, repair his boat, and wait for more favorable conditions before giving it a go once again.

The 2017 crossing proved to be incredibly difficult, with unrelenting winds and strong currents making it almost impossible for the Pole to make progress at times. On occasion, he would paddle all day long, just to maintain his current position. In the early going, Doba found himself drifting farther away from his intended course, heading in a more southerly direction rather than east as he had planned. Those were long, lonely days for the solo kayaker, who thought that he might have to abandon his attempt to cross the Atlantic yet again when his rudder broke during a powerful storm. Fortunately, a passing ship helped him correct the problem and eventually he was able to maneuver his twenty-three-foot custom-built kayak into an ocean current that would propel him all the way to Europe, eventually making landfall in France.

We can take a lot away from Doba's story, including the fact that he first embarked on these kinds of epic adventures at a relatively later stage in his life. Paddling across an ocean at any age is a serious undertaking, but doing it for the first time at sixty-five is especially impressive. That was the goal that the Polish adventurer had set for himself however, and he wasn't about to let anything stand in his way. He certainly wasn't going to use age as an excuse for not trying either.

The business world is also filled with a number of well-documented examples of men and women who went on to become major success stories in the later stages of their careers. For instance, Ray Kroc founded McDonald's when he was fifty-two, turning it into a global brand that is recognized and loved by millions around the world. Sam Walton didn't open his first Wal-Mart store until he was forty-four, and yet he still had plenty of time to turn his company into the largest retailer in the world within his lifetime. Similarly, Henry Ford didn't perfect the design of his Model T automobile until he reached the age of forty-five, and that was only the start of what he would accomplish. He would also go on to introduce the concept of an assembly line to the manufacturing process, while also creating the V8 engine and building the first truly modern factory.

Author J. K. Rowling was thirty-two years old when she published the first book in her Harry Potter series. That isn't especially old of course, but considering the circumstances of her life at the time, it would have been easy for her to think that she had missed her window of opportunity to become a writer.

She first came up with the idea for the enormously popular series of books when she was just twenty-five, but in the years that followed she faced a number of obstacles that delayed her road to success. Not only did her mother pass away, but Rowling was married, divorced, and became a single mom all in the span of just a few years. She even found herself on welfare for a time while she studied to become a teacher and get her life together.

Despite these challenges however, Rowling continued to work on her first novel, spending time in coffee shops and working late into the evening while her young daughter was asleep. Eventually she was able to put together three full chapters of the book and began submitting it to publishers. The reception was lukewarm at best, however, with more than a dozen companies choosing to pass on Harry Potter and his magical world.

Despite the steady stream of rejection letters arriving in her mailbox, Rowling remained committed to her goal of seeing her book published. When yet another rejection letter arrived, she'd tack it to the refrigerator door to serve as reminder to work harder and not give up. And while there were no doubt times when she wondered if she'd ever catch a break, she always found a reason to keep writing and hoping that someday she might be able to walk into a bookstore and see her creation on the shelves.

Eventually a London publishing house agreed to publish Rowling's book after the daughter of its chairman read the first few chapters and begged to know what happened next. That same chairman gave Rowling a modest advance for writing the rest of the novel, but advised her to get a day job, too. He apparently saw no future for her as a writer, but as it turns out he needn't have worried all that much.

As we all know, Harry Potter was a gigantic success, spawning six sequels, eight Hollywood blockbuster movies, and an award-winning play. Rowling's story sparked the imagination of young and old alike, selling more than 400 million copies worldwide. The amazing reception for the franchise was enough to earn its author more than $1 billion, making her the most financially successful writer in history.

While struggling to get her career on track, it would have been easy for Rowling to just give up. Jobless, recovering from the loss of her mother and a difficult divorce, all while caring for a young child, no one would have blamed her for setting aside her ambitions to be an author to focus on other things. But she never lost faith in her own ability, nor did she let fear keep her from going after her goals. In the end, despite all of the adversity and doubt, she was able to persevere and her story stands as an inspiration to millions of others.

While some people see time as something that is continually slipping away, others see it as a resource that is plentiful. So much so that they continue putting off the pursuit of their goals because they work under the assumption that they'll have lots of time to get around to doing the things that they truly want to do at a later date. They tell themselves that they'll chase that goal once they've become more established in their careers, started a family, and settled into a typical routine. Those are all obviously good things that are worth focusing on, provided we don't allow them to become yet another crutch that keeps us from reaching the other goals that we've always had for ourselves too.

I've always felt that one of the greatest tragedies in life is not death, but what we let die inside of us while we still live. Yes, establishing a family, getting your career on track, and enjoying your favorite activities are all important aspects of life. But they don't have to be the death of your dreams, too.

There is a well-known quote that says "no one who is on their deathbed has ever said I wish I had spent more time at the office." Instead, we typically tend to regret the things we didn't do in our lives rather than the things we've actually done. We end up wishing that we had spent more time with friends and family or that we had traveled more. We wish that we had actually spent more time away from the office, doing the things that are ultimately more important and rewarding. And yes, we end up wishing we had run that marathon, started that business, or wrote that book.

One modern day adventurer who didn't want to go through her life always wondering what could have been is Roz Savage. A solo ocean rower from the UK, Savage dramatically altered the course of her life after spending more than a decade working as a management consultant in London. In that line of work, her hours were long, the stress levels were high, and recognition was often fleeting. And while the pay may have been good, the other rewards were few and far between.

Savage was always a driven student who generally scored high marks in her classes. She was also instilled with a sense of curiosity and wonder about the world around her. She attended Oxford where she graduated with a law degree and distinguished herself as a member of the rowing team. Post-university, she settled into a regular life, complete with a high paying job in the city and a comfortable house in the suburbs.

As the years past, Roz started to wonder if there was anything more to life than just grinding out a living by working in London. All she ever seemed to do was go to work, come home, and try to seek out a little adventure when she could find the time. Then one day while riding the train to her office she decided to try a little experiment. She began to write two obituaries for herself—one that was written from the perspective of the life she was currently living, while the other came from the life she truly wanted to lead. They were not at all similar to one another, and she was startled by what she had read. It was then that she knew she had to make a change.

Not long after that, she quit her job and went looking for other things to fuel her passions. For instance, she joined a three-month long expedition to explore Inca ruins in Peru. She returned home long enough to write a book about that experience, before signing on as part of the crew of a sailing yacht. But ultimately she found her calling at a gathering of members of the Royal Geographical Society in London—the UK equivalent of the famed Explorers Club in the US.

It was there that Roz met Daniel Byles, who told her about the challenges he faced while rowing across the Atlantic Ocean with his mother a few years earlier. Savage hung on his every word, becoming intrigued with the idea without even fully understanding the challenges that she might face. The thought of being all alone out on the ocean for weeks on end was both thrilling and inspiring at the same time. She wanted to know what it was like to live on a rowboat for weeks at time surrounded by nothing but open water in all directions.

Not long after her chance meeting with Byles, Savage committed herself to following in his footsteps and rowing across the Atlantic completely on her own. She decided to take part in an annual rowing race that started in the Canary Islands off the coast of North Africa and ended nearly 3,000 miles later in the West Indies in the Caribbean. She was the only woman who entered the race as a solo competitor that year, but she was determined to finish no matter what Mother Nature threw at her while out on the water.

After deciding she was ready to take on this ambitious new challenge, Savage put the project management skills she had learned in her previous career to good use and set about attracting sponsors and financial supporters to her cause. She also put in a healthy chunk of her own money to build a state of the art rowboat complete with solar panels to provide power, a desalination system to create fresh drinking water, and a GPS navigation system to help her find her way.

Eventually she was ready, and in 2005 Savage set out on her

journey across the Atlantic, which was everything she had hoped for and so much more. It took her 103 days to cover the entire distance and when she was done she became the first woman to row solo as part of the Atlantic Rowing Race. But achieving that wasn't easy; while out on the ocean she broke all four of her oars, had her cook stove stop functioning just three weeks into the voyage, and lost satellite communication twenty-four days before she reached the finish line. Despite all of those setbacks however, she just kept pushing forward.

For most people, successfully rowing across one ocean would be enough of an adventure to last a lifetime, but Roz was only getting warmed up. She followed up her Atlantic row by making a solo crossing of the Pacific in three stages spread out across 2008, 2009, and 2010. That journey covered more than 8,000 miles between California and Papua New Guinea and took 250 days to complete, making her the first woman to row the Pacific completely on her own. In 2011, she would add the Indian Ocean to her resume, spending 154 days at sea while covering more than 5,000 miles between Australia and Mauritius. It was her longest single journey yet.

For now, Roz has hung up her oars to concentrate on new challenges, most notably working to protect the Earth's oceans from environmental threats. She started a nonprofit organization that is dedicated to that task, while she also serves as an author and motivational speaker. That is a far cry from her former career as a management consultant, which would have certainly taken her down a completely different path. Savage has said on more than one occasion that "life can be so fulfilling if you can only figure out what it is you want to do."

While quitting her job and completely upending her lifestyle worked very well for Roz Savage, it obviously isn't the right answer for everyone. Still, there is a lot we can learn from her story. For instance, Savage was able to set some monumental goals for herself and then figure out a way to achieve them. She was also courageous enough to completely abandon a safe and secure—albeit unfulfilling—life in order to go after the one that she truly wanted for herself. That isn't an easy decision to make when you've already charted a course down a lucrative and comfortable career path, particularly when friends and family can't always understand why you would want something different. Savage wasn't afraid to push herself beyond her own boundaries, both physically and mentally, while chasing after her dream of a more adventurous and fulfilling lifestyle. And she has demonstrated that she possesses, as we say in the SEAL Teams, a "Combat Mindset" by being able to spend more than 520 cumulative days at sea completely alone.

If you're looking for further proof that it is never too late to start chasing your goals, no matter how lofty they might be, look no further than director James Cameron. Arguably the most successful filmmaker of all time, Cameron has given us such films as *Titanic*, *The Terminator*, and *Avatar*, all of which have been monster hits. The success of his blockbuster movies has made Cameron one of the busiest and most sought-after talents in all of Hollywood, with every film, documentary, and television show that he produces garnering plenty of media attention. Of course, all of his success has made him millions of dollars along the way and afforded him the ability to pick and choose the projects that he wants to work on, both professionally and personally.

You would think that a guy like James Cameron would have enough on his plate to keep him busy on a constant basis. But, he is an intelligent, passionate, and driven individual who has goals that go far beyond just making his next movie. In fact, his side projects have taken him to places that few other human beings have ever gone, putting him in the most rarified air imaginable.

In 1989, Cameron made a film called *The Abyss*. The story centered around a team of petroleum engineers working with the US government to recover a sunken submarine before the Russians could get their hands on it. While plumbing the depths of the ocean, they encounter an alien race that has been hiding beneath the surface, monitoring our progress as a species. At the time of its release, the film was lauded for its special effects and exceptional realism, even winning the Academy Award for Best Visual Effects.

In order to make the film feel as realistic as possible, Cameron studied the intricacies of traveling to great depths under the water.

He learned everything there was to know about SCUBA gear, atmospheric diving suits, and deep-sea submersibles—something that would also come in handy when he made *Titanic* a few years later. The director went to great lengths to make *The Abyss* look as accurate as possible, while also offering up some near-future technology that hadn't necessarily been completely perfected yet. Along the way he also managed to become a bit of an expert on deep-sea exploration, which would eventually generate a whole new set of macro-goals for him.

After *The Abyss* was released, Cameron moved on to other projects, producing a string of hits that only further cemented his reputation as one of the most bankable filmmakers in the business. And while there was always a new movie on the horizon, there was also a germ of an idea in his head that he just couldn't seem to shake. After learning so much about what it takes to visit the deepest parts of the ocean, Cameron began formulating a plan that would allow him to visit the very depths that he had depicted in his film. That meant plunging into the Mariana Trench—the deepest point on our planet at 35,756 feet below sea level. To put that into perspective, Mt. Everest could be dropped into the trench and there would still be 6,700 feet above its summit to spare.

Years past as Cameron continued working on films and television shows, all the while thinking about his goal of going to a place that only two other human beings had ever been. The so-called Challenger Deep sat in the heart of the Trench, more than six miles beneath the surface of the ocean. It had only been visited by man on one occasion, with Navy Captain Don Walsh and Swiss engineer Jacques Piccard making that historic journey back in 1960. The duo descended into the ocean in a tiny submarine custom built to survive the enormous pressures exerted on anything that ventured into that inhospitable place. At the time, it was a gigantic scientific endeavor on par with going to the moon. Aside from a few remotely operated vehicles, no one had ever been back to the Challenger Deep since.

In 2009, Cameron released *Avatar*, which would become the biggest box office success in history. Naturally, there was immediate demand from the public—not to mention the studio that released the film—for a sequel, but the director had other things in mind. He had already decided that his next project was to make his goal of visiting the bottom of the ocean a reality. In order to do that he secretly went to work with an Australian engineering company to build a submersible vehicle that could take him into the Mariana Trench and hopefully return him to the surface safely. It would take about eighteen months to design and construct the vehicle, which would be christened the Deepsea Challenger.

For a test run, Cameron took the Challenger to the bottom of the New Briton Trench, making a solo descent to a depth of over five miles. The vehicle performed exactly as he had expected, clearing the way for his real goal—the Challenger Deep.

On March 26, 2012—more than twenty-three years after he had filmed *The Abyss*—James Cameron descended into the Mariana Trench at long last. He spent three hours exploring the deepest place on the planet, mapping the underwater terrain, collecting sediment samples, and gathering a wealth of data. And while he was only there for a brief time, he managed to discover sixty-eight new species of bacteria and small invertebrates.

When Cameron made his historic dive he was fifty-seven years old, a time in most people's lives when they're looking to slow down and take things a bit easier. He had just finished producing the biggest film in the history of cinema and had countless studio executives pressuring him to reveal what it was he wanted to do next. His life was as busy as ever, and yet he still found time to not only pursue a personal goal, but also make history in the process. That personal goal wasn't something as simple as losing a few pounds or taking up running or cycling. It was to go to one of the most remote and dangerous places on the planet. Perhaps we should ask ourselves what exactly is keeping us from pursuing our goals?

The point of these stories is that there is never a time in your life that isn't right for defining and pursuing new goals, regardless of how big or small they might be. Finding success isn't limited by how old you happen to be when you begin, which is why Mozart could write a symphony at the age of eight and famed artist Grandma Moses didn't start painting until she was in her seventies.

As human beings, we're quick to find excuses for why we shouldn't even try to pursue new and meaningful goals. We tell ourselves we're too busy, we're too tired, or we're too old—because that's exactly what some of us want to believe. The reality is, if you want something bad enough you'll actually make it a priority, sacrificing things that aren't as important in order to achieve your goal. Sometimes, finding success is a matter of choosing between what you want now, and what you want more.

There are numerous training programs available to help beginning runners prepare for their first race. These programs generally have a schedule that starts slowly and builds up distance and duration over time. In the beginning, a runner will spend just three or four hours a week as part of the routine, increasing their stamina and getting accustomed to exercising a few miles at a time. But as they make their way in the program, the mileage they cover starts to increase, just as their speed and endurance increases. Eventually, they'll reach a peak training period just a few weeks before the race, after which they'll start to taper off from their training and enter a recovery phase. At the peak of a beginner training program, many athletes may only be running about ten to twelve hours per week, which in the grand scheme of things isn't a major commitment, particularly if the goal it to actually run a marathon.

According to the Nielsen ratings, the average American watches more than thirty-five hours of television each and every week of the year. As if that wasn't enough, comScore—a company that measures media consumption—indicates that in 2017 a typical American adult spends nearly three hours a day on their smartphone. Any way you look at it, that's a lot of time spent in front of a screen that could be used for other activities.

If we focused on shaving a few hours off our television viewing and smartphone habits, we could certainly free up some extra time in our schedule for other things. For instance, by cutting back the time we spend watching TV to just twenty hours a week—which still equates to nearly three hours of television per day—we would find ourselves with fifteen additional hours freed up to pursue more meaningful goals. That's plenty of time to train for a marathon, learn a new skill, write a business plan, or work on whatever project you've been dreaming about.

If you take a look at your own life, chances are, you'll find some extra time in your schedule that can be channeled towards something positive and meaningful. It could be getting up earlier on the weekend to focus on writing your first novel or skipping happy hour with friends to hit the gym instead. We all have the same number of hours in our day, but successful people are often just a little bit more efficient in how they use them.

There is a famous quote—often misattributed to Mark Twain—that says, "Twenty years from now, you will be more disappointed by the things you didn't do than by the ones you did do. So throw off the bowlines. Sail away from the safe harbor. Catch the trade winds in your sails. Explore. Dream. Discover."

In the end, it doesn't really matter who actually said it because those are excellent words to live by. They are a reminder that we should pursue all aspects of our lives with passion and discipline or we may just end up regretting all of the things we let slip away. Regret is a bitter pill to swallow, but thankfully it is one that we don't necessarily have to taste. When we sail way from our "safe harbors" we can truly start to understand all that we are capable of achieving, and perhaps we'll gain the confidence, conviction, and mindset needed to reach further than we ever imagined.

Personally, I never wanted to be someone who ended up saying, "I should have helped more people, I should have done more, I should have tried harder, I should have given more, I should never have let go of the dreams" Instead, I want to be—and will be—the person who says, "I did not succeed at all I attempted, I did not do well at some of the things I did, but at least I tried. I pushed myself to my full potential and achieved most of what I set out to accomplish."

If we all approach life with that can-do attitude and mindset, we can accomplish great things. There will be few boundaries that we can't push past and fewer goals that will truly be out of our reach. If we can at least say that we gave it our all, and pushed ourselves to our full potential, achieving most of what we set out to do, we will all have lived a full life indeed. In the end, that just might be the biggest and best goal of all.

Do not let this void go unfulfilled. Reach for your full potential. If you stay at "conversational pace" for your entire life, you may be comfortable, but you will leave this big part of the triangle empty. Race pace hurts more but you will accomplish so much more while operating in that zone. As part of the SEAL Teams we did not have the luxury at training at conversational pace—it was race pace or nothing at all.

On the other hand, you can't exist at race pace forever. You can use it as a tool to help you become laser-focused on achieving a particular goal, but after you've given it your all, you have to back off, take a break, and give yourself a chance to prepare for your next objective.

I once believed that I constantly needed to push myself and my teammates well beyond the "line." That way I could ensure that we were giving it our all. On a monthly basis, for well over a decade, I would push myself to the point of hallucinations, vomiting, bonking, bleeding, and/or passing out. I pushed myself so hard one year that my liver and kidneys almost shut down and I went from weighing more than 180 pounds to less than 140 pounds in a very short period of time. My body "ate from itself" and it almost killed me.

I no longer would ever encourage anybody to push themselves that hard. It is very dangerous and could easily result in injury or death. Beyond that, in other facets of our life, family issues can arise from too much stress, neglect, and other factors. Now, I know the secret. Go up to your limits, just touch that line, and then back off. Don't go into the preverbal "Death Zone."

But, if you stay in the "Comfort Zone" for too long, your life will go by and at the end of it all, you will not have accomplished all that you could have. We need to push ourselves beyond our boundaries and out of that comfort zone from time to time, or we simply won't achieve everything that we want to in life.

There is one thing we all have in common: one day we are going to wake up to find that time has run out. Whatever you do, don't let time take your dreams away.

EPILOGUE

"A climber is not intimidated by a mountain—but inspired by it. The winner is not discouraged by a problem—but challenged by it. Mountains are created to be conquered; adversities are designed to be defeated; problems are sent to be solved. It is better to master one mountain than a thousand foothills."
                                                    —William Ward

Throughout the course of this book, I have shared some wild tales from my own life and from the lives of others. I've tried to use these stories to not only entertain and inform, but also serve as examples of how we can all push through the boundaries that hold us back in our lives. Hopefully, the concepts that I've illustrated here can help you along the road to achieving your goals.

As for me, I know that my life would have gone nowhere if it were not for developing a powerful mindset—a Combat Mindset. If I had not been so goal driven, I never would have gotten as much out of life as I have. Earlier in this book (see Chapter 4), I highlighted many of the macro-goals I had set for myself and have accomplished along the way. Now and in the future, my life will continue down that same path by constantly strengthening my mindset and setting monumental macro-goals for myself.

I turned sixty years old in 2017 and feel so very blessed and fortunate to have survived my near-death experience on Everest the year before. Numerous other climbers who also suffered from high altitude pulmonary and cerebral edema did not make it off the mountain and some of their bodies are still there frozen in place. That could have been me, and while I was disappointed that I was unable to achieve my goal of reaching the summit of Everest, my experience there was a sharp reminder to continue pursuing the life that I want to live for as long as I can.

When I came home, I set a new macro-goal for myself. My plan is to ride my bicycle, at sea-level, on flat roads, at sixty miles per hour. I call this the Sixty at Sixty Challenge. Sixty years old, sixty miles per hour. This may or may not be an age group record, I don't know, nor do I care. What is important to me is that I keep this flame alive and do not get too comfortable, lazy, or allow myself to feel too old. My long term macro-goal is to continue living the life I love. It is as simple as that.

I firmly believe that the most powerful weapon on Earth is the human soul on fire. Driven by passion and a desire to push ourselves further than we've ever gone before can allow us to do great things. If I'm able to complete my Sixty at Sixty Challenge, it would be the fastest that I have ever ridden a bike in my life. As a life-long cyclist, that is a thrilling thought and I look forward to taking on this endeavor.

I was just recently selected to take part in what was an amazing adventure during which I, and a group of nine teammates, set out on a seven-week, 750-mile paddle and hike over the Rockies in northern Canada. This expedition was filmed for a new television show which will air in Canada and in the US. The entire journey was self-navigated and self-propelled. I wouldn't have it any other way.

As you can tell, I haven't stopped setting new macro-goals for myself, nor will I ever choose to do so. There are still so many things that I want to accomplish in my lifetime. So many adventures yet to discover.

It is my hope that I've helped send others down a similar path and that they too pursue their own dreams, and never stop pushing beyond their own boundaries.